WILD REVIEW

Season 2021/22

Season summaries, match reports, photos and statistics for the Wild NIHL team, Widnes Ladies and Academy Under 10, 12, 14, 16 and 18 teams as told in the pages of the Widnes Weekly News during the 2021/2022 season

ICE HOCKEY REVIEW

www.icehockeyreview.co.uk

Interesting Books...
...Fascinating Subjects!
Publishing
www.poshupnorth.com

Publishing History

The majority of the season reviews and match reports in this book have been previously published on the www.widneswild.co.uk website and in the Widnes and Weekly News and Runcorn newspapers.

The lists of fixtures / results, league tables and player statistics are based on information taken from the eiha.co.uk and Fixtures Live websites, although they have not been published anywhere in this layout before.

This edition published in Great Britain in July 2022 by Ice Hockey Review, which is an imprint of Posh Up North Publishing, Beckenham Road, Wallasey, United Kingdom

ISBN: 978-1-909643-51-2

Cover Photos

Front Cover: The Wild NIHL team celebrate winning the Moralee Cup in March 2022 (Photo by Geoff White)

Back Cover: Author Paul Breeze presenting the MVP award to Preston Gennoe after the Wild Ladies' WPL game against Nottingham Vipers in November 2021 (Photo by Geoff White)

LIST OF CONTENTS

PB presenting the MVP award to Preston Gennoe after the Wild Ladies' WPL game against Nottingham Vipers in November 2021 (Photo by Geoff White)

INTRODUCTION

If, when flicking through this book, you get that "déjà lu" feeling that you have read a lot of this before, well you probably have.

A lot of the stories reproduced here have either appeared online on the Widnes Wild website, or in print in the local Widnes Weekly News – or quite possibly both.

But, having written thousands and thousands of words about the various Widnes ice hockey teams over the past season, it seemed a bit of a shame to leave them merely consigned to being chip paper (do they still use newspaper for wrapping chips in...?) or hovering helpless in the ether at the mercy of some cyber terrorist who could delete everything on the internet on a whim at the flick of a switch...

So I decided, therefore, to preserve this mighty volume of work for the benefit of future generations of ice hockey fans, players, statisticians and historians in the shape of a book – and that is what you are now looking at.

So, if you happen to be sitting on a desert island with no internet access, or at home in the middle of a power cut, or – maybe - in the dusty and unfortunate aftermath of some very unpleasant apocalyptic occurrence, you can still read up on the YKK Widnes Wild's highly impressive debut 2021/22 season in the NIHL North Moralee Division and relive the excitement of the 3rd place finish and the Cup win all over again.

There is also full coverage of the Wild Ladies team's roller-coaster - and, indeed, record breaking - season in the Women's Premier League - and all of the Wild Academy teams from Under 18s down to Under 10s.

How many goals did Vlads Vulcanovs score in the group stages of the Moralee Cup? It's in here!

Who were the only team to come away with a result from Dumfries all season? That's in here as well.

Who scored the Wild's first goal in the away win at Solihull on 18th December? That too.

Who were the Wild Ladies MVP awards named in memory of this season...? And that.

Plus a lot of other interesting facts such as who won the YKK banner design competition and what is the difference between SA% and GAA....?

All of that makes it quite a hefty book, for which I make no apologies. After all, look how big the Encyclopaedia Britannica is and there's not even hardly any ice hockey in that!

You can never have enough books (says the independent book publisher with a completely straight face...) and you can certainly never have enough ice hockey books.

So, if you are a fan of British ice hockey, NIHL ice hockey in particular or just ice hockey in general, I am sure you will find something to interest you here.

Paul Breeze,
Wallasey, July 2022

YKK Widnes Wild Team Photo – Season 2021/22
Back Row: Louis Rosslyn (Eqp Mgr), Wez Spurrett (General Manager) Tom McDonald (Netminding Coach), Keiron Furlong, Ken Armstrong, Dani Haid, Chris Wilcox, Tristan Grimshaw, Tom Stubley, Vlads Vulkanovs, Lee Kemp, Jay Robinson, Jakub Hajek, Joe Greaves, Joe Wyatt, Liam Charnock, Cain Taylor, Ben Larnach (Physio), Bob Bramah (Head Physio), Nigel Thorpe (Physio), Megan Hughes (Physio) Front Row: Evan Coles, Tom Brierley, Nathan Britton, Mikey Gilbert, Tom Jackson, Harrison Walker, Richard Haggar (Player Coach), Bez Hughes, Kieran Beach, Jack Murray, Oliver Goodman. (Photo by Geoff White – www.gw-images.com)

Widnes Wild Season Review 2021/22 by Paul Breeze

The YKK sponsored Widnes Wild had their best ever season in terms of league performance, having finished the 2021/22 campaign in 3rd position in their first ever season in the Moralee Division.

It was a superb achievement for player coach Richard Haggar and his new look team and back room staff – especially as they also won the Moralee Cup, seeing off stiff opposition in the group stage, overcoming Solway Sharks in the semi-final final and then beating Dundee Comets over two legs in a closely contested final.

The Wild entered the season as the new boys in the division but they already had a growing reputation at the higher level after a successful mini season in the "behind closed doors" streaming series saw them secure the North 21 Cup and the National Division 1 Championship Title.

However, a full length league season playing against long-established teams was a different prospect all together and Haggar had the daunting task of putting together a squad that would be able to consistently compete at that level.

Many of the old fan favourites from the Laidler Division team returned for the new season and they were boosted by signings from Hull Jets such as Kieran Beach, Jay Robinson and Tom Brierley, along with Sheffield sharpshooter Nathan Britton, Vlads Vulcanovs and Joe Wyatt from Altrincham and, later in the year, Matty Barlow from Bradford.

The Wild also attracted major National Division talent with the signings of Chris Wilcox and Tom Stubley from Hull Pirates and Liam Charnock from Leeds Chiefs and all three went on to be key players for the season.

In goal, Harrison Walker continued the fine form that he showed in the streaming series games and Evan Coles has been a very worthy back up. The Wild also encouraged youth development with the signing of several under-23 players on 2 way contracts with Laidler Division teams, all of whom had the opportunity to play in Moralee matches this season.

In terms of their playing record for the season, it is probably fair to say that Widnes exceeded most people's expectations.

To notch up home and away wins on a consistent basis against long established Moralee Division sides such as Solihull Barons, Billingham Stars, Blackburn Hawks – and even the fast improving Nottingham Lions - is not to be sniffed at.

The Wild even managed to run eventual league champions Solway Sharks close in their various encounters, taking a point for an overtime league loss at home and then drawing 3-3 away in the cup semi final, which was the only time that the Sharks failed to win in Dumfries all season.

Widnes then beat Solway 5-4 in the home leg of the cup semi-final to set up a fascinating two-legged final against Dundee Comets.

The final followed a very similar pattern to the semi with Widnes drawing 3-3 away on Tayside on the Saturday and then securing the cup with a narrow 4-3 win at home the night after.

Back in the league, eventual runners up Whitley Warriors were the only other real fly in the ointment this season with 4 straight wins in 4 league games – and one of those games went to overtime and a penalty shoot out after a 3-3 draw on Merseyside.

So, following a barnstorming first season in the Moralee Division, the Wild finished in a very creditable 3rd place in the league table – with 35 points from their 28 games.

This left them 8 points adrift of second place Whitley and a massive 18 behind champions Solway – but also a good 8 points ahead of 4th place Solihull Barons.

A final record of 16 wins and 3 overtime losses at this level is a very impressive achievement and is a great basis to build upon for next season.

Top Points Scorers

In the scoring stakes, Vlads Vulcanovs was the top goalscorer in the Moralee Division with 38 goals in 26 league games while Richard Haggar notched up the most assists – 42 from 28 games.

Peter Gapa from Solway Sharks was the top overall points scorer with 33+34 while Haggar and Vulcanovs finished up 3rd and 4th with 18+42 and 38+21 respectively.

In terms of the Widnes team, Liam Charnock weighed in with 9+24, Tom Stubley with 11 + 21 and Matty Barlow, Chris Wilcox, Dani Haid, Mikey Gilbert, Nathan Britton, Joe Greaves & Jay Robinson all reached double figures.

Penalty Kings

Joe Greaves ended up with the highest penalty minutes on the Widnes roster with 101 PIM from 16 games, finishing behind Craig Lutkevitch (Blackburn – 122 PIM), Zachary Yokoyama (Nottingham - 120 PIM) and level with the Hawks' Reece Cairney Witter.

In fairness to all of these players, it should be pointed out that following a change in the rules on fighting penalties for the 2021/22 season, the EIHA scoring online system was left with an anomaly where a 5 minute fighting penalty had to be recorded as a "5 + Game" even when no additional game penalty was awarded.

This glitch means that some of the player penalty counts for this 2012/22 season are over-inflated and not entirely accurate.

Top Netminder

In the league netminder standings, the Wild's Harrison Walker finished as the league's top goalie with a 91.36% save percentage from 27 league matches, narrowly ahead of Whitley Warriors' Dean Bowater with 91.12%.

Evan Coles ended up with a very creditable 83.23 SA%, bearing in mind that he had never played at this level before.

Play Offs

Unfortunately, the end of season play offs did not go the way of the Wild and Widnes were knocked out in the quarter-final by Billingham – who they had beaten 4 times out of 4 during the regular season.

A change of format for this season's play offs saw all 8 teams in the Moralee Division take part in a knock-out round to decide the 4 semi finalists. The pairings were decided by final league placings with 1st v 8th, 2nd v 7th etc and this saw 3rd place Widnes matched against 6th place finishers Billingham Stars.

Under the previous arrangements, the top 4 finishers in the league would have gone straight through to the Play Off weekend in Leeds and Widnes would have played Whitley Warriors in the semi final, giving them another chance to get one over on their north east nemesis.

However, quarter-final knock outs it was and, on this occasion a funny thing happened at the Forum as Widnes had a rare "bad day at the office" and Billingham built up a huge 8-1 lead to carry over to the second leg.

That left too much of a deficit to make up in the return game – even for Widnes – and the 3-2 win gave the Wild a victory on the night but they failed to make the play off weekend for the first time in their history – which took a bit of the shine off an otherwise highly impressive and successful season.

Vlads Vulcanovs (#13) was the Moralee Division's top goal scorer with 38 goals, while Richard Haggar (#19) had the most assists with 42 (Both photos by Geoff White)

NIHL MORALEE DIVISION 2021/22

Final Table	GP	W	OW	OL	L	PIM	F	A	Pts
Solway Sharks	28	24	2	1	1	341	177	82	53
Whitley Warriors	28	18	3	1	6	360	143	82	43
Widnes Wild	28	15	1	3	9	422	125	114	35
Solihull Barons	28	12	0	3	13	357	142	119	27
Sheffield Scimitars	28	10	0	4	14	356	109	121	24
Billingham Stars	28	9	2	0	17	273	102	122	22
Blackburn Hawks	28	4	5	0	19	632	127	205	18
Nottingham Lions	28	6	1	2	19	517	88	168	16

Leading Scorers	Team	GP	G	A	Pts	PIM
Peter Gapa	Solway Sharks	21	33	34	67	8
Niklas Ottosson	Solihull Barons	20	21	40	61	34
Richard Haggar	Widnes Wild	28	18	42	60	14
Vlads Vulkanovs	Widnes Wild	26	38	21	59	12
Petr Valusiak	Blackburn Hawks	27	24	32	56	30
Thomas Soar	Solihull Barons	26	32	21	53	29
Chris Sykes	Billingham Stars	28	23	28	51	14
Zachary Yokoyama	Nottingham Lions	27	29	21	50	120
Scott Henderson	Solway Sharks	23	20	28	48	21
Louie Andrew Newell	Nottingham Lions	25	20	28	48	65

Top Netminders	Team	GP	SA	GA	SA%	SO
Harrison Walker	Widnes Wild	27	984	85	91.36%	0
Dean Bowater	Whitley Warriors	23	484	43	91.12%	3
Thomas Brown	Billingham Stars	27	1066	100	90.62%	0
Calum Hepburn	Solway Sharks	26	556	54	90.29%	0
James Hadfield	Sheffield Scimitars	22	758	75	90.11%	1
Sam Hewitt	Solihull Barons	26	538	61	88.66%	0
Graham Laverick	Solihull Barons	26	434	58	86.64%	2
Luca Sheldon	Nottingham Lions	26	813	120	85.24%	1
Michael Rogers	Blackburn Hawks	28	1071	160	85.06%	0
Matthew Bloor	Nottingham Lions	21	301	45	85.05%	2

The Wild's Harrison Walker (#32) was the top performing netminder in the Moralee Division for the 2012/22 Season (Photo by Geoff White)

Notes on Netminder Statistics

Unfortunately the official netminding figures provided by the by the EIHA on Fixtures Live are based solely on Save Percentage (SA%) and don't necessarily take into account how much time a netminder has spent in goal.

This means that if a netminder plays just 10 minutes in goal all season, faces 10 shots and lets 1 goal in, he will probably end up with a better SA% then a regular first choice netminder who performs well in every game he plays.

There is a separate calculation of netminder performance called Goals Against Average (GAA) which takes the total of number of minutes that a netminder has stood in goal divided by the number of goals that has conceded and averaged out by dividing by 60 minutes to arrive at an average goals per game figure.

The application of this calculation instead of – or alongside – SA% often arrives at a different set of results for the same netminder standings.

In the case of our illustrative "10 minute netminder", he would end up with a GAA of 6 BUT he would not make the final standings in the first place because there is usually a minimum requirement of minutes to be stood in goal – say 640 - so as not to skew the figures.

Generally speaking, the application of the GAA figure could be viewed as a fairer way of assessing and comparing the performance of netminders who make a lot of appearances over the course of a season.

Fixtures & Results - Season 2021/22

Date	Match	Home			Away	Res
05/09/2021	Ch	Widnes Wild	10	2	Sheffield Titans	W
11/09/2021	M Cup	Blackburn Hawks	5	4	Widnes Wild	L
12/09/2021	Moralee	Widnes Wild	4	7	Whitley Warriors	L
19/09/2021	Moralee	Nottingham Lions	2	7	Widnes Wild	W
25/09/2021	M Cup	Sheffield Scimitars	8	9	Widnes Wild	W OT
03/10/2021	Moralee	Billingham Stars	3	4	Widnes Wild	W
09/10/2021	Moralee	Solway Sharks	5	1	Widnes Wild	L
10/10/2021	M Cup	Widnes Wild	6	4	Sheffield Scimitars	W
17/10/2021	M Cup	Widnes Wild	8	2	Blackburn Hawks	W
23/10/2021	Moralee	Sheffield Scimitars	8	0	Widnes Wild	L
24/10/2021	M Cup	Solihull Barons	5	7	Widnes Wild	W
31/10/2021	M Cup	Widnes Wild	2	7	Solihull Barons	L
07/11/2021	Moralee	Whitley Warriors	7	4	Widnes Wild	L
14/11/2021	Moralee	Widnes Wild	4	1	Billingham Stars	W
28/11/2021	Moralee	Widnes Wild	5	6	Solway Sharks	L OT
05/12/2021	Moralee	Widnes Wild	7	2	Nottingham Lions	W
11/12/2021	MCSF1	Solway Sharks	3	3	Widnes Wild	D
12/12/2021	MCSF2	Widnes Wild	5	4	Solway Sharks	W
18/12/2021	Moralee	Solihull Barons	4	5	Widnes Wild	W
19/12/2021	Moralee	Widnes Wild	3	2	Sheffield Scimitars	W OT
09/01/2022	Moralee	Blackburn Hawks	5	4	Widnes Wild	L OT
16/01/2022	Moralee	Widnes Wild	3	4	Blackburn Hawks	L
22/01/2022	Moralee	Sheffield Scimitars	2	1	Widnes Wild	L
23/01/2022	Moralee	Widnes Wild	8	5	Nottingham Lions	W
30/01/2022	Moralee	Widnes Wild	2	5	Solway Sharks	L
06/02/2022	Moralee	Nottingham Lions	3	4	Widnes Wild	W
13/02/2022	Moralee	Widnes Wild	6	4	Solihull Barons	W
19/02/2022	MCF1	Dundee Comets	3	3	Widnes Wild	D
20/02/2022	MCF2	Widnes Wild	4	3	Dundee Comets	W
27/02/2022	Moralee	Widnes Wild	3	4	Whitley Warriors	L OT
05/03/2022	Moralee	Solihull Barons	2	6	Widnes Wild	W
06/03/2022	Moralee	Whitley Warriors	8	2	Widnes Wild	L
12/03/2022	Moralee	Solway Sharks	9	3	Widnes Wild	L
13/03/2022	Moralee	Widnes Wild	8	4	Solihull Barons	W
20/03/2022	Moralee	Blackburn Hawks	3	8	Widnes Wild	W
26/03/2022	Moralee	Widnes Wild	5	2	Blackburn Hawks	W
27/03/2022	Moralee	Widnes Wild	5	2	Billingham Stars	W
03/04/2022	Moralee	Billingham Stars	2	4	Widnes Wild	W
10/04/2022	Moralee	Widnes Wild	9	3	Sheffield Scimitars	W
16/04/2022	POFFQ1	Billingham Stars	8	1	Widnes Wild	L
17/04/2022	POFFQ2	Widnes Wild	3	2	Bilingham Stars	W

Key:
Ch = Challenge Match
M Cup = Moralee Cup Group Stage
Moralee = Moralee Division
MCSF = Moralee Cup Semi Final

MCF = Moralee Cup Final
POFFQ = Play Off Quarter Final
POFFS = Play Off Semi Final
POFFF = Play Off Final
OT = Over Time Win / Loss

Wild Player Statistics - Moralee Division

Player	GP	G	A	Pts	PIM
Richard Haggar	28	18	42	60	14
Vlads Vulkanovs	26	38	21	59	12
Liam Charnock	25	9	24	33	43
Thomas Stubley	28	11	21	32	60
Matthew Barlow	22	9	10	19	14
Chris Wilcox	28	0	16	16	21
Daniel Haid	21	8	7	15	2
Michael Gilbert	17	7	7	14	8
Nathan Britton	26	6	5	11	2
Joe Greaves	16	3	7	10	101
Jay Robinson	17	4	6	10	35
Thomas Jackson	25	0	6	6	6
Kieran Beach	7	3	2	5	0
Tom Brierley	23	0	5	5	22
Lee Kemp	23	1	4	5	46
Jakub Hajek	3	2	2	4	4
Berwyn Hughes	19	3	1	4	2
Josh Reynolds	9	1	3	4	2
Ken Armstrong	23	0	2	2	2
Harrison Walker	27	0	2	2	0
Keiron Furlong	24	1	0	1	6
Tristan Grimshaw	22	0	1	1	2
Jack Murray	27	0	1	1	10
Joe Wyatt	19	1	0	1	2
Evan Coles	20	0	0	0	0
Oliver Goodman	8	0	0	0	0
Jake Lowndes	1	0	0	0	0
Cain David Taylor	1	0	0	0	0

Netminder	GP	SA	GA	Sv%	SO
Harrison Walker	27	984	85	91.36%	0
Evan Coles	20	167	28	83.23%	0

MORALEE CUP 2021/22

Midlands Group	GP	W	OW	OL	L	PIM	F	A	Pts
Solihull Barons	6	4	0	0	2	117	38	26	8
Widnes Wild	6	3	1	0	2	44	36	31	8
Sheffield Scimitars	6	3	0	1	2	62	43	29	7
Blackburn Hawks	6	1	0	0	5	54	18	49	2

North Group	GP	W	OW	OL	L	PIM	F	A	Pts
Solway Sharks	6	6	0	0	0	89	27	16	12
Dundee Comets	6	4	0	0	2	95	20	14	8
Whitley Warriors	6	2	0	0	4	140	20	20	4
Billingham Stars	6	0	0	0	6	113	16	33	0

Semi Final 1
11th Dec: Solway 3 – Widnes 3
12th Dec: Widnes 5 – Solway 4
Widnes win 8-7

Semi Final 2
Dundee 5 – Solihull 0
Solihull 0 – Dundee 5
Tie awarded to Dundee

Final - First Leg
19th Feb: Dundee 3 – Widnes 3

Final - Second Leg
20th Feb: Widnes 4 – Dundee 3

Widnes win 7-6 on aggregate

MORALEE PLAY OFFS

Q/ finals: 2 legged ties played home and away on 16th & 17th April.

Quarter Final 1
Billingham 8 – Widnes 1
Widnes 3 – Billingham 2
Billingham win 10-4

Quarter Final 2
Blackburn 0 – Whitley 3
Whitley 18 – Blackburn 2
Whitley win 21-2

Quarter Final 3
Solway 7 – Nottingham 2
Nottingham 0 - Solway 7
Solway win 14-2

Quarter Final 4
Sheffield 3 - Solihull 5
Solihull 6 – Sheffield 2
Solihull win 11-5

Play Off Weekend - at Planet Ice Leeds, 23rd & 24th April
SF1: Solway 6 - Billingham 2   **SF2:** Whitley 4 – Solihull 1
Final: Solway Sharks 5 – Whitley Warriors 2

Div 1 National Final (At Coventry, 1st May)
Solway Sharks 4 – Streatham 2

Wild Player Statistics – Moralee Cup

	Group		Semi - F		Final		Cup Totals				
	GP	Pts	GP	Pts	GP	Pts	GP	G	A	Pts	PIM
Vlads Vulkanovs	6	19	2	6	2	2	10	16	11	27	6
Richard Haggar	6	15	2	3	2	3	10	8	13	21	6
Liam Charnock	5	9	2	2	2	4	9	5	10	15	12
Thomas Stubley	6	9	2	2	2	4	10	3	12	15	8
Kieran Beach	6	12	0	0	0	0	6	5	7	12	6
Chris Wilcox	6	6	2	2	2	1	10	0	9	9	8
Michael Gilbert	3	6	2	1	2	0	7	1	6	7	2
Nathan Britton	6	5	1	0	2	0	9	3	2	5	0
Jay Robinson	6	2	2	1	2	1	10	1	3	4	4
Joe Greaves	0	0	2	3	2	1	4	2	2	4	31
Tom Brierley	4	2	2	0	2	0	8	0	2	2	13
Daniel Haid	2	0	2	0	2	2	6	2	0	2	0
Keiron Furlong	5	1	2	0	2	0	9	1	0	1	2
Tristan Grimshaw	6	1	2	0	2	0	10	1	0	1	0
Jakub Hajek	4	1	0	0	0	0	4	1	0	1	2
Jack Murray	4	1	2	0	2	0	8	0	1	1	2
Joe Wyatt	6	1	0	0	1	0	7	0	1	1	25
Matthew Barlow	0	0	0	0	2	1	2	1	0	1	6
Ken Armstrong	6	0	2	0	2	0	10	0	0	0	0
Evan Coles	5	0	0	0	2	0	7	0	0	0	0
Oliver Goodman	2	0	0	0	0	0	2	0	0	0	0
Berwyn Hughes	1	0	0	0	2	0	3	0	0	0	0
Thomas Jackson	4	0	2	0	2	0	8	0	0	0	0
Lee Kemp	5	0	1	0	2	0	8	0	0	0	6
Cain Taylor	2	0	0	0	0	0	2	0	0	0	0
Harrison Walker	4	0	2	0	2	0	8	0	0	0	0
Josh Reynolds	0	0	0	0	1	0	1	0	0	0	0

Netminder		GP	SA	GA	Sv%
Evan Coles	Group	5	102	12	88.24%
Harrison Walker	Group	4	158	19	87.97%
	Semi	2	85	7	91.76%
	Final	2	73	6	91.78%
	Totals	8	316	32	89.9%

Wild Player Statistics – Moralee Play Offs

Player	GP	G	A	Pts	PIM
Liam Charnock	2	1	3	4	28
Vlads Vulkanovs	2	1	1	2	6
Michael Gilbert	2	0	1	1	2
Richard Haggar	2	1	0	1	0
Berwyn Hughes	2	1	0	1	2
Thomas Stubley	2	0	1	1	0
Ken Armstrong	2	0	0	0	0
Matthew Barlow	2	0	0	0	0
Tom Brierley	2	0	0	0	4
Nathan Britton	1	0	0	0	0
Keiron Furlong	2	0	0	0	0
Oliver Goodman	2	0	0	0	0
Joe Greaves	2	0	0	0	11
Tristan Grimshaw	2	0	0	0	0
Daniel Haid	2	0	0	0	0
Thomas Jackson	2	0	0	0	6
Lee Kemp	2	0	0	0	0
Jack Murray	2	0	0	0	0
Josh Reynolds	2	0	0	0	0
Harrison Walker	2	0	0	0	0
Chris Wilcox	2	0	0	0	0
Joe Wyatt	1	0	0	0	0

Netminder	GP	SA	GA	Sa%	SO
Harrison Walker	2	80	10	87.50%	0

Widnes Wild Player Statistics
All Matches – Season 2021/22

Player	League GP	League Pts	Play Offs GP	Play Offs Pts	Cup GP	Cup Pts	Chall GP	Chall Pts	Totals GP	Totals G	Totals A	Totals Pts	PIM
Vulkanovs	26	59	2	2	10	27	1	3	39	55	36	91	24
Haggar	28	60	2	1	10	21	1	3	41	28	57	85	22
Charnock	25	33	2	4	9	15	1	1	37	16	37	53	83
Stubley	28	32	2	1	10	15	1	3	41	14	37	51	68
Wilcox	28	16	2	0	10	9	1	1	41	0	26	26	29
M Gilbert	17	14	2	1	7	7	1	2	27	9	15	24	12
M Barlow	22	19	2	0	2	1	0	0	26	10	10	20	20
K Beach	7	5	0	0	6	12	1	3	14	10	10	20	6
D Haid	21	15	2	0	6	2	0	0	29	10	7	17	2
N Britton	26	11	1	0	9	5	1	1	37	10	7	17	2
J Greaves	16	10	2	0	4	4	1	2	23	7	9	16	143
Robinson	17	10	0	0	10	4	1	1	28	6	9	15	39
TBrierley	23	5	2	0	8	2	1	0	34	0	7	7	39
J Hajek	3	4	0	0	4	1	1	2	8	3	4	7	6
T Jackson	25	6	2	0	8	0	1	0	36	0	6	6	12
L Kemp	23	5	2	0	8	0	1	0	34	1	4	5	52
B Hughes	19	4	2	1	3	0	1	0	25	4	1	5	4
Reynolds	9	4	2	0	1	0	0	0	12	1	3	4	2
Grimshaw	22	1	2	0	10	1	1	1	35	2	1	3	2
Armstrong	23	2	2	0	10	0	0	0	35	0	2	2	2
Walker	27	2	2	0	8	0	1	0	38	0	2	2	0
Furlong	24	1	2	0	9	1	0	0	35	2	0	2	8
Wyatt	19	1	1	0	7	1	1	0	28	1	1	2	27
Murray	27	1	2	0	8	1	1	0	38	0	2	2	12
Coles	20	0	0	0	7	0	0	0	27	0	0	0	0
Goodman	8	0	2	0	2	0	0	0	12	0	0	0	0
Lowndes	1	0	0	0	0	0	0	0	1	0	0	0	0
Taylor	1	0	0	0	0	0	0	0	1	0	0	0	0

Netminder		GP	SA	GA	Sv%
Evan Coles	Moralee	20	167	28	83.23%
	Cup	5	102	12	88.24%
	Total	**25**	**269**	**40**	**85.10%**
Harrison Walker	Challenge	1	15	2	86.67%
	Moralee	27	984	85	91.36%
	Cup	8	316	32	89.90%
	Play Offs	2	80	10	87.50%
	Total	**38**	**1395**	**129**	**90.80%**

Wild v Titans face off shot (Photo by Geoff White)

Sunday 5th September 2012 – Challenge Match
YKK Widnes Wild 10 – Sheffield Titans 2

The YKK sponsored Widnes Wild got the new 2021/22 NIHL season off to a winning start with a 10-2 challenge match victory over the Sheffield Titans at Planet Ice Widnes on Sunday.

It was the first senior game to be played in front of fans at Widnes for 18 months due to the Covid lockdowns and a keen crowd was in attendance to see player coach Richard Haggar's new-look Wild team.

Widnes debuts were handed to Tom Brierley, Nathan Parkes-Britton, Vlads Vulkanovs, Joe Wyatt, Chris Wilcox, Evan Cole, Tom Stubley, Cain Taylor, Jack Murray, Liam Charnock and Kieron Furlong and this game was a good opportunity for them to gel with the returning Wild players before the competitive season starts in earnest next week.

The opposing Titans team are a new outfit who were only formed in the summer as a development side to allow younger players from the Sheffield Academy to gain senior league experience on a regular basis.

They have filled the gap left in the lower Laidler Division by the Sheffield Scimitars who have moved up to join the Wild in the Moralee Division this time around. It was the Titans' first ever game of any sort and, with the best will in the world, coming up against a team packed with players with NIHL National Division experience, the final result was always likely to be a foregone conclusion.

The Wild took the lead just 90 seconds into the game with a debut strike from Nathan Britton and there then followed a tense phase where Widnes continued to put pressure on the Sheffield goal, without managing any further breakthrough. The second goal finally came after 16 minutes from Kieran Beach and the score remained at 2-0 at the first period break.

The home side edged further ahead with a goal from Joe Greaves on 26 minutes but they were then caught out with two quick fire goals from the Titans to pull the score back to 3-2. Jay Robinson buried the puck in the net for the Wild to get them back on track just two minutes later and second strikes for both Beach and Greaves rounded off a highly entertaining 6-goal second period.

The match was well and truly killed off with 4 more Widnes goals in the first 5 minutes of the third period – from Liam Charnock, Mikey Gilbert, Tristan Grimshaw and Richard Haggar.

New Wild netminder Evan Cole replaced Harrison Walker in goal for the final 20 minutes and the game petered out somewhat as Widnes eased off in the latter stages.

The post-match presentations were made by Eleanor Manson-Sawko, Business Development Manager for Halton Haven Hospice - who are the Wild's chosen charity for the season - and the MVPs went to netminders Harrison Walker and Nicholas Winters for the Wild and Titans respectively.

New Wild Captain for the season Tom Jackson and Alternate Captains Mikey Gilbert and Bez Hughes were also presented with the NIHL North Cup, which the Widnes team had won in the behind closed doors competition earlier in the year.

Widnes Wild v Whitley Warriors (Photo by Geoff White)

Saturday 11th September 2021 – NIHL Midlands Cup
Blackburn Hawks 5 -   YKK Widnes Wild 4

Sunday 12th September 2021 – NIHL Moralee Division
YKK Widnes Wild 4 – Whitley Warriors 7

The YKK sponsored Widnes Wild had an eventful opening weekend of the new NIHL 2021/22 season, putting in two battling performances but losing 5-4 away in the Midlands Cup to Blackburn Hawks on Saturday and then 4-7 at home in the league to Whitley Warriors at Planet Ice Widnes on Sunday.

The game in East Lancashire on Saturday saw Richard Haggar's new look Widnes team come up against a lot of familiar faces in the Blackburn line up as, due to the relatively close proximity, there has been a lot of interchange of players over the years and these games are always very keenly contested.

The opening stages were very tense – with both teams testing each other out and neither wanting to give anything away – and it took until the 17th minute before former Wild player Lee Pollitt gave Blackburn the lead.

Tom Stubley equalised for Widnes just 90 seconds later but a further strike for the Hawks just 45 seconds after that handed the home side a 2-1 lead at the first period break.

The second period was just as close and pretty much the same thing happened as another former Wild player – Matt Wainwright - edged Blackburn further into the lead on 37 minutes and then new Widnes import – Latvian Vlads Vulkanovs - pulled a goal back just a minute later. However, Pollitt was on target once again for Blackburn with just three seconds left in the period to leave the score standing at 4-2 to the Hawks.

The third period saw the Wild move up a gear and two goals within 90 seconds of each other – from Vulkanovs and then Nathan Britton - saw them pull level with 15 minutes still to play. Unfortunately, they were unable to build further on this positive spell and the score remained deadlocked at 4-4 as the clock slowly ticked down.

The decisive blow came with just under two minutes left to play when Blackburn scored what turned out to be the winning goal – interestingly enough from another former Widnes player, Michal Novak.

The home game on Sunday - at home to reigning champions Whitley Warriors in front of a sell-out crowd - got off to a dream start for the Wild with a goal from Keiron Furlong after just 33 seconds.

The Warriors got into their stride, however and equalised on 9 minutes and then edged into the lead just 90 seconds later with a powerplay goal.

Two more goals for Whitley gave them a 1-4 lead at the first period break but Widnes were giving a good account of themselves in their first ever Moralee Division game and there was still plenty to play for.

The next goal also went to the visitors - on 24 minutes - and then a sixth goal at the half way point of the game looked as if might have put the game out of the Wild's reach. However, heads did not drop and a shorthanded goal from Vlads Vulkanovs on 33 minutes followed up by a superb strike by player coach Richard Haggar halved the deficit and raised hopes of a Widnes fightback.

Whitley bounced back with another goal on 37 minutes to make the score 3-7 and then shut up shop for the night. Widnes looked better as the game went on and managed to outshoot the visitors by 17 to 16 in the third period but the Warriors' defence was very stubborn and it took until the 57th minute of the game before the Wild were able to breach it again.

A second goal of the night for Vulkanovs rounded off the scoring – handing the Wild a 1-0 "win" for the period - and the game finished 4-7 to the Warriors.

Looking back at the weekend games, Wild Player Coach Richard Haggar said:

"Both games where close contests and could have gone either way. On Saturday against Blackburn, the game was end to end and no doubt was a good spectacle for the fans."

"We picked up a couple of injuries in the first 2 periods when we were already short benched but this seemed to galvanise the team and due to an unfortunate call disallowing a goal which would have put us 5-4 ahead with a few of the game to go seemed to change the game back in Blackburn's favour."

"The Sunday we started very slowly and were 4-1 down in the first period but then matched them in the second and third but again a short bench and injuries picked up through Sunday didn't help our cause."

"It was certainly a learning curve in to D1 hockey for myself and the team but there was certainly a lot of positives to take from the games. Being down in both games but never giving up until the final whistle is what we will continue to show in every game we play this season and hopefully turn these close games around to wins for the Wild."

Wild Player Coach Richard Haggar (#19) in action away at Nottingham
(Photo by Richard Davies / Chud Photography)

Sunday 19th September 2021 – NIHL Moralee Division
Nottingham Lions 2 - YKK Widnes Wild 7

The YKK sponsored Widnes Wild picked up their first Moralee Division win of the season (and, in fact, ever - as this is their first campaign competing in the higher division) with a 2-7 victory away to Nottingham Lions on Sunday.

Battles between the two "big cats" have always been memorable encounters over the years and it was important that Widnes put in a good display on this occasion as Nottingham have traditionally struggled since stepping up a league and have been the whipping boys of the division in recent seasons.

Despite the fairly comprehensive final scoreline, this game was actually very close for much of the time and could easily have gone either way. There were no goals in the first period and it took until the 26th minute for the first breakthrough, which came courtesy of the Wild's Vlads Vulkanovs, who scored on a delayed penalty call.

Widnes went two goals up five minutes later with a second strike from Vulkanovs but the Lions pulled a goal back just 90 seconds later to keep themselves in the game.

A second goal for the hosts with just over a minute to go in the period levelled up the score, leaving the match finely balanced at 2-2 with 20 minutes left to play.

Widnes upped their game considerably in the third period and were notably the better side. They outshot the Lions by 19 to 8 and killed the game off with five unanswered goals.

The first of these came from player coach Richard Haggar just 4 minutes into the period and then Mikey Gilbert doubled the lead on 47 minutes.

A strike from Nathan Britton and a brace from Jakub Hajek sealed the win for the Wild and the 2-7 result saw them climb to third place in the Moralee Division table at this early stage of the season.

There was a bit of steam letting off right at the end with under a minute left on the clock as Wild's Joe Greaves got involved in an enthusiastic punch up with Zachary Yokoyama of the Lions, which resulted in both of them being sent to the penalty box for the last few seconds of the game.

No sooner had this "bout" finished then Jay Robinson left the Wild bench for what appeared to be a pre-orchestrated tussle with Lions' Ben Wilson and, once the pair of them had fallen to the ice in a heap, they were both banished to the dressing rooms. Ironically enough, the game had not been overly rough and the 100 minutes dished out for those 4 players at the end accounted for all but 12 of the total penalties handed out for the whole game.

Saturday 25th September 2021 – Moralee Midlands Cup
Sheffield Scimitars 8 – Widnes Wild 9 (OTW)

The YKK sponsored Widnes Wild picked up a sensational 8-9 victory with a dramatic over time win away to the Sheffield Scimitars in the Moralee Midlands Cup on Saturday.

This was the first meeting between the two teams since Widnes had beaten Sheffield in the National Division 1 Championship final and with both teams playing up in the higher division for the first time, it always seemed likely to be a closely fought game.

Sheffield took the lead after just 28 seconds of the game but Widnes equalised just 3 minutes later with a goal from Vlads Vulkanovs. A second Scimitars strike right at the end of the period handed them a narrow 2-1 lead heading into the break and a third goal three minutes from the restart edged them further ahead.

Keiron Furlong halved the deficit for Widnes on 28 minutes and 3 minutes later Kieran Beach fired home to level the scores. Two goals late in the second period saw Sheffield leading 5-3 heading into the final 20 minutes but Widnes were looking very strong and there was still plenty to play for.

The Scimitars got themselves into penalty trouble early in the third period and the Wild were quick to punish these infringements. A powerplay gaol from Vulkanovs in the 44th minute narrowed the gap to just one goal and then a second powerplay strike just 30 seconds later from Mikey Gilbert levelled the score once more.

Then just 21 seconds after that, Wild player coach Richard Haggar fired home to put Widnes into the lead for the first time in the game.

Sheffield fought back with two goals to retake the lead and when the Scimitars lost a man to the penalty box on 55 minutes, Widnes called a time-out to discuss tactics. Whatever was discussed obviously worked as the Wild's former Sheffield player Nathan Britton fired in a powerplay goal just 36 seconds from the puck drop to level the score at 7-7.

The last few minutes were agonising to watch as the clock slowly ran down and both teams closed up to try and avoid making a costly last minute error.

Then with 40 seconds left in the game, Sheffield scored their 8th goal and looked as if they had done enough to secure the match. Widnes, undaunted, pushed forward and, with just 19 seconds to play, Vulkanovs fired in his hat trick goal to force the game into over time.

With Tom Stubley in the box for interference, Widnes went into the 5 minute over time period with a man disadvantage but the tables were turned 90 seconds into extra time once Stubley had returned to the fray and the Scimitars were assessed a hooking penalty. The game was decided after 3 minutes 31 seconds of sudden death over time with a golden goal from Nathan Britton to hand Widnes a hard-fought and well deserved 8-9 victory

Despite the win, Widnes remain bottom of the Midlands Cup group table with 1 win from their 2 games to date, level on points with Blackburn Hawks, who have played one game more. Sheffield receive a point for the Over Time Loss and head the table with 5 points from 3 games

Wild away at Billingham (Photo by Linda Crabtree)

Sunday 3rd October 2021 – Moralee Division
Billingham Stars 3 – YKK Widnes Wild 4

The YKK sponsored Widnes Wild made it three wins in three games with a sensational 3-4 win away at Billingham Stars in the Moralee Division on Sunday.

This was the first time that Widnes had ever won a game against Billingham and puts them in a promising position in the league table at this early stage of the new season.

The Wild took the lead in the 7th minute with a goal from Tom Stubley and held that advantage - despite being outshot in the first period by 23 to 16 – until the 18th minute when Billingham equalised on a powerplay. However a superb goal from Kieran Beach in the last minute of the period handed Widnes a narrow 1-2 lead at the first break.

The Wild lead was further extended two minutes from the restart with a goal from player coach Richard Haggar and Widnes were leading 1-3 as the game approached its midway point.

The Widnes momentum was disrupted somewhat as Haggar took a stick to the face and had to leave the ice for treatment. There was a brief stoppage for blood to be cleared off the playing surface and the Stars player involved received a 2+2 minute penalty for high sticks.

Unfortunately, the Wild were not able to make the most of their 5 on 4 advantage and Billingham pulled a goal back on 32 minutes. The score remained 2-3 to Widnes heading into the final period and the game was very much on a knife-edge.

With a patched-up Haggar returned to the fray, Widnes looked very strong in the third period as they looked to protect their lead but, unfortunately for them, Billingham fired in an equaliser on 50 minutes, setting up a dramatic finale.

In a very tense third period – during which Widnes outshot the hosts by 10 to 8 - the decisive moment came in the 54th minute when Mikey Gilbert scored for the Wild to secure their first ever win in the North East.

The win sees Widnes move up to third place in the Moralee Division table with two wins from their three league games to date.

They sit comfortably just two points behind leading pair Solway Sharks and Whitley Warriors – and can look forward to a visit to Dumfries to take on the league leaders this Saturday 9th October.

Following their trip north of the border, the Wild will play their first home fixture in almost a month when they take on the Sheffield Scimitars in the Midlands Cup on Sunday 10th October at Planet Ice Widnes – 5.30 pm face off.

Harrison Walker (#32) Tom Stubley #56 and Jack Murray (#71) defend the Wild goal away at Solway (Photo by Helen Hobbins Photography)

Saturday 9th October 2021 – Moralee Division
Solway Sharks 5 – YKK Widnes Wild 1

The YKK sponsored Widnes Wild lost 5-1 away to Moralee Division league leaders Solway Sharks in Dumfries on Saturday.

The game was pretty close in the first period as both teams sat back and tested each other out and it remained deadlocked until the hosts opened the scoring in the 17th minute to lead 1-0 at the first break.

Solway scored again in the 22nd minute and got a third just 90 seconds later. Then an incident in the 34th minute saw the Wild assessed a 2 minute bench penalty for too many men on the ice and Tom Stubley ejected from the match with a 5+game call for boarding.

This left the Wild facing a 5 on 3 powerplay for two minutes and then a 5 on 4 for the rest of Stubley's 5 minutes and, after bravely holding out for 1m50sec, they eventually succumbed to a powerplay goal which gave the Sharks a 4-0 lead.

While the Wild didn't look outclassed by any means, they left themselves too much to catch up on in the third period and Solway fired home again to make the score 5-0 5 minutes into the third period.

Widnes finally found the back of the net with a consolation strike from Lee Kemp with 5 minutes left on the clock.

The Mayor of Halton – Cllr Christopher Rowe – drops the puck before the Widnes v Sheffield match (Photo by Geoff White)

Sunday 10th October 2021 – Moralee Midlands Cup
YKK Widnes Wild 6 – Sheffield Scimitars 4

The YKK sponsored Widnes Wild moved up into second place in the Midlands Cup group table after a highly entertaining 6-4 win over the Sheffield Scimitars at Planet Ice Widnes on Sunday.

Widnes took the lead in the 7th minute with a goal from Jay Robinson and then doubled the advantage with a strike from player coach Richard Haggar just 35 seconds later.

The score remained 2-0 to Widnes at the first period break but Sheffield pulled a goal back just two minutes from the restart to keep themselves in contention. The game see-sawed somewhat at this point and could have gone either way

But three unanswered goals for Widnes – two from Kieran Beach and a short handed strike from Vlads Vulkanovs in between – put the Wild well and truly in the driving seat with a 5-1 second period lead.

A 6th goal from Liam Charnock just 84 seconds into the third period looked to have it sewn up for the Wild but Sheffield fought back with two quick goals to leave the score standing at 6-3 to Widnes with 15 minutes still to play.

A powerplay play goal for the Scimitars with just 80 seconds to go made for a nerve-wracking finish to the game but Widnes held on to secure a 6-4 victory.

The win means that Widnes are now second in the Midlands Cup group table at the half way stage of the "round robin" games. They are just one point behind group leaders Sheffield, who have played two games more and could go top if they beat Blackburn Hawks in their next game - which is this Sunday 17th October at Planet Ice Widnes, 5.30pm face off.

After the game, the Wild Player Of The Month award for September was presented to Vlads Vulkanovs. The winner was decided by the fans via an online Twitter poll.

The Mayor of Halton - Cllr Christopher Rowe - was a special guest at the match and was on hand to help unveil the winning design in the recent Kit Colouring Competition. The competition had been organised by Wild main sponsors YKK and the prize was to have the winning design made into a banner to be displayed at Wild home games. The winning design was submitted by James Walker.

James Walker shows off his winning design with Wild players Liam Charnock (#21), Nathan Britton (#10) and Tom Stubley (#56). (Photo by Geoff White)

Wild sheriff Lee Kemp (#15) and Hawks enforcer Reece Cairney Witter come to blows in the North West derby match (Photo by Geoff White)

Sunday 17th October 2021 – Moralee Midlands Cup
YKK Widnes Wild 8 – Blackburn Hawks 2

The YKK sponsored Widnes Wild moved to the top of the Midlands Cup group table after a superb 8-2 win over north west rivals Blackburn Hawks at Planet Ice Widnes on Sunday.

The Wild had previously beaten the Hawks home and away in the recent streaming series games but those matches were played behind closed doors - so this was the very first time that Widnes had beaten Blackburn on home ice in a rink full of fans and was, therefore, a memorable occasion for the yellow camp.

Meetings between Widnes and Blackburn are always passionate and exciting affairs and, this is augmented by the fact that, due to the close proximity between the two teams, there has always been a lot of interchange of players over the years.

The Hawks team this season – with former Widnes head coach Mike Clancy at the helm – has several former Wild players on their roster including : Matthew Wainwright, Tom Revesz, Calum Ruddick, MJ Clancy, Michal Novak, Lee Pollitt and former Riverside Raiders rec netminder Mike Rogers, while the Wild line up includes former Blackburn players Ken Armstrong, Harrison Walker, Jack Murray, Joe Greaves and Keiron Furlong.

Widnes took the lead in the 8th minute with a goal from Kieran Beach but Blackburn hit back with an equaliser from Jared Dickinson on 14 minutes.

Just when it looked as if the game would be tied at the first period break, Blackburn scored again – with Dickinson's second goal of the night with just 47 seconds left on the clock - to give them a narrow 1-2 lead after 20 minutes of play.

Right at the start of the third period, Wild netminder Harrison Walker over-stretched when diving to make a save, pulling a muscle, and he had to be replaced by back up Evan Coles. This was Coles' first appearance in goal for the Wild this season, but you would never know as he put in a blinding performance.

Widnes equalised with a powerplay goal from Latvian import Vlads Vulkanovs on 27 minutes and then a brace from player coach Richard Haggar on 31 and 37 minutes put them in a promising 4-2 lead by the end of the second period.

The third period continued in similar vein with the Wild putting Blackburn under intense pressure and outshooting them by an incredible 22 to 8.

A goal from Jakub Hajek extended the lead on 43 minutes and then a superb short handed strike from Vulkanovs on 46 minutes made the score 6-2 to Widnes.

Things got a bit niggly in the closing phase of this game and Blackburn turned physical to vent their frustrations, picking up 14 of their 18 penalty minutes during the third period.

Tom Stubley fired the Wild further ahead in the 49th minute and, shortly afterwards, the crowds were entertained by a fight between Wild "Sheriff " Lee Kemp and Blackburn's keenly pugilistic captain, Reece Cairney-Witter that let off some of the steam that had been building between the two teams.

The scoring was rounded off for Widnes with a 58th minute goal from youngster Tristan Grimshaw – his first competitive senior goal for the

Wild, with an assist for former Hawks player Jack Murray, representing his first point for Widnes since joining in the summer.

In the 39 minutes and 47 seconds that he was in goal, back up netminder Evan Coles did not let a single shot past him and he was rightly named Most Valuable Player of the game for Widnes, while the accolade for Blackburn went to Mike Rogers in the Hawks goal.

The win puts Widnes top of the Midlands Cup group table with 2 games left to play.

Both of their remaining games are against the Solihull Barons with the away game coming this Sunday 24th October and the home game the following Sunday 31st October at Planet Ice Widnes.

Two wins for Widnes over the Barons would secure them the Midland Cup outright and also a place in the semi finals against the top teams from the North Cup qualifying group.

Before that, the Wild have a tricky away game to negotiate in the league against Sheffield Scimitars on Saturday 23rd October at iceSheffield – 4pm face off.

Vlads Vulkanovs (#13) finds the net against Blackburn Hawks (Photo by Geoff White)

Wild captain Tom Jackson robustly defends the Widnes goal away at Solihull
(Photo by Keith & Jenny Davies)

Sunday 24th October 2021 – Moralee Midlands Cup
Solihull Barons 5 – YKK Widnes Wild 7

The YKK sponsored Widnes Wild consolidated their position at the top of the Moralee Midlands Cup group table with a thrilling 5-7 win away to Solihull Barons on Sunday.

The result was the perfect response to the disappointing 8-0 shut out away to Sheffield in the league on Saturday evening and means that Widnes can win the Midlands Cup if they beat Solihull at home in their next game on 31st October.

The game started badly for the Wild, with Solihull rushing to a 3-0 first period before Liam Charnock eventually opened the Widnes account on 17 minutes. Charnock fired in another with just 48 seconds left in the period and the score stood at 3-2 at the first break.

Widnes scored first in the second period, with Vlads Vulkanovs levelling on 22 minutes, but the Barons re-took the lead two minutes later.

Another exchange of goals saw Wild player/coach Richard Haggar equalise on 25 minutes, only to have Solihull take the lead once more. Then - just as it looked as if the home side would take a narrow lead into the second break - Kieran Beach fired in a powerplay goal for Widnes to level the score at 5-5.

This game was really close fought, with the two teams very well matched throughout, and it really could have gone either way. After a tense opening to the third period, Widnes finally got the breakthrough and took the lead for the first time in the game with a goal from Haggar on 46 minutes.

The latter stages of the game got a bit niggly and there were several penalties handed out to both sides. However, Solihull came out the worst in these interruptions in play and all it did was hamper their chances of a late fightback.

Still chasing a 1-goal deficit as the game entered its final two minutes, the Barons withdrew their netminder in favour of an extra attacker but the tactic backfired and Liam Charnock sealed the win for Widnes with an Empty Net Goal at 59.32.

The win keeps the Wild top of the group table with 8 points from 5 games and one match left to play.

Sheffield Scimitars are in second with 5 points from 5 games but, even if they win their remaining game, they will not be able to overtake Widnes.

Solihull still have two games to play and could mathematically still catch the Wild if they win both of those - but a victory for Widnes in their home game against the Barons on Sunday would be enough to guarantee them the trophy.

The Wild are now also guaranteed a place in the cross-over semi finals for the separate NIHL North cup competition where they will meet the top finishing teams in the Moralee North cup group table. At present, those two slots are occupied by Solway Sharks and Whitley Warriors, but there are still a number of matches to be played in that competition.

The YKK sponsored Wild are next in action this Sunday 31st October when they take on the Solihull Barons in the Midlands Cup at Planet Ice Widnes. Doors open at 4.45 and face off is at 5.30pm.

Saturday 23rd October 2021 – Moralee Division
Sheffield Scimitars 8 – YKK Widnes Wild 0

The YKK-sponsored Widnes Wild had a frustrating trip away to Sheffield on Saturday, losing out 8-0 to the Scimitars in the Moralee Division at iceSheffield.

On paper this should have been a fairly close game with both teams locked on the same number of points and having a similar playing record for the season so far. In fact, Widnes had already beaten Sheffield twice this season so this rather one-sided result stands out as a bit of an anomaly.

The Wild did not play badly and actually had more of the play. Over the course of the game they outshot Sheffield by 45 to 30 but whatever they tried, the puck simply would not go in the net. At the other end, the Scimitars seemed to have no such problem with scoring and took each period 2-0, 4-0, and 2-0.

Widnes had a man advantage on 7 separate occasions over the course of the game due to Sheffield players being in the penalty box. However, the resulting powerplays did not produce any breakthroughs and, in fact, they conceded two short handed goals within 28 seconds of each on 27 minutes.

So this was very much a night to forget for the Wild. These things happen from time to time in ice hockey and they just need to put it behind them and regroup ready to face the further challenges ahead.

Widnes Wild v Solihull Barons (Photo by Geoff White)

Sunday 31st October 2021 – Moralee Midlands Cup
YKK Widnes Wild 2 – Solihull Barons 7

The YKK sponsored Widnes Wild missed out on the opportunity to secure top spot in the Midlands Cup Group following a 2-7 home defeat at the hands of Solihull Barons at Planet Ice Widnes on Sunday.

A win for the Wild would have seen them finish top of the group - with the benefit of an easier draw in the semi-finals of the overall Moralee Division cup competition but, with a game still in hand, the Barons will be able to overtake them if they win their last group game against Blackburn Hawks.

As it was Halloween night, there was a party atmosphere around the rink with prizes for the best costumes provided by team apparel sponsors Cross Check Clothing – but very little of the surrounding good cheer found its way onto the ice.

Solihull opened the scoring 4 minutes into the game but Widnes equalised with a goal from Latvian forward Vlads Vulkanovs midway through the period and the score remained 1-1 at the first break.

This was quite an even contest up to now and the next breakthrough didn't come up until the 26th minute while the Wild were a man short due to a tripping call – their only penalty of the whole game.

Solihull scored on the resulting powerplay and then went further ahead on 34 minutes to lead 1-3 after two periods.

Any hopes that the Wild had of salvaging anything from the game were dashed when Solihull scored their 4th goal 5 minutes into the period – and then fired in 3 more unanswered strikes to build up a commanding 1-7 lead by the 53rd minute.

A second Widnes goal did eventually come from the stick of Vulcanovs on 55 minutes on a boarding powerplay but by then it too late to inspire much of a fightback and the game finished 2-7 to Solihull.

There were a few scuffles that broke out on the ice after the final buzzer as tensions that had built up between the players over the course of the game began to boil over - and the teams were despatched to the dressing rooms before the MVP awards were announced to prevent any serious escalation.

Once order had been restored, the Post Match presentations went to Tom Stubley for Widnes and netminder Sam Hewitt for Solihull.

Following this result, Solihull move up into second place in the Cup Group table – 2 points behind Widnes but with a game in hand. The Wild are already confirmed a place in the semi finals - which will be played against the top two finishing teams in the NIHL North Cup Group - but the Barons, if they don't win their last group game next Sunday, could still be overtaken by Sheffield Scimitars who also have a game left to play against the Blackburn Hawks.

In terms of the scoring standings for the Midlands Cup Group, the Wild's Vlads Vulcanovs is currently top with 11 goals and 8 assists from the 6 games all together. Richard Haggar is second with 6+9 and Kieran Beach is third with 5+7, level with Solihull's Thomas Soar.

The Wild are next in action this Sunday 7th November when they travel away to take on the Whitley Warriors in the Moralee Division – 5pm face off.

They are next at home the following Sunday 14th November when they entertain Billingham Stars at Planet Ice Widnes.

Widnes Wild away to Whitley Warriors (Photo by Pyro Media)

Sunday 7th November: Moralee Division
Whitley Warriors 7 – YKK Widnes Wild 4

The YKK sponsored Widnes Wild put in a battling performance away to league leaders Whitley Warriors on Sunday before finally succumbing 7-4 in the North East.

The reigning champions from the Covid-curtailed 2019/20 season took the lead on 3 minutes and then doubled the advantage some 5 minutes later but a strike from Joe Wyatt - his first of the season - just 45 seconds after that opened the account for the Wild.

A third goal followed for Whitley on 16 minutes but two quick goals for Widnes – in the last minute of the period – from Kieran Beach and Tom Stubley - dramatically tied the score at 3-3 at the first break.

By the half way point of the game, the score was still 3-3 and Widnes were giving a good account of themselves in their first ever league match away at Whitley Bay

However, they were unable to break through the stubborn Warriors' defence and the home side scored twice more to lead 5-3 after two periods.

A powerplay goal from Liam Charnock on 44 minutes narrowed the gap to just one goal but that was as good as it got for Widnes as two unanswered strikes from Warriors' top goal scorer this season, Latvian import Rolands Gritans, completing his hat trick, put the game beyond the reach of the battling Wild.

A fight between the Wild's "Sheriff" Lee Kemp and Whitley's Jordan Barnes livened up an otherwise low key final few minutes and both players received a 5+game for their troubles. Interestingly enough, apart from a 2 minute call for hooking to the Warriors earlier in the third period these were the only penalties handed out in the whole match.

Despite the win, the Warriors are knocked off the top of the Moralee Division table after Solway Sharks notched up a 4-point weekend with wins over Nottingham and Billingham. Both teams have 14 points but the Sharks are top by virtue of a better playing record against Whitley.

Widnes are currently 7th in the league table with 4 points from 6 games but they have played fewer matches than most of the other teams.

The Wild are next in action this Sunday 14th November when they take on the Billingham Stars at Planet Ice Widnes – 5.30 pm face off. It is Remembrance Sunday so there will be a minute's silence before the game and the charity Help For Heroes will be in attendance.

Wild's Vlads Vulkanovs (#13) scores against Billingham (Photo by Geoff White)

Sunday 14th November 2021 – Moralee Division
YKK Widnes Wild 4 – Billingham Stars 1

The YKK sponsored Widnes Wild got back to winning ways with a 4-1 Moralee Division win over Billingham Stars at Planet Ice Widnes on Sunday.

As the game was played on Remembrance Sunday, there was 2 minutes silence with bugle calls before the game and representatives from the Help For Heroes charity were in attendance.

The first period was goal-less - which is quite unusual for an ice hockey match – although Widnes had the more chances, outshooting the visitors by 18 to 10.

The breakthrough finally came on 24 minutes when Latvian import player Vlads Vulkanovs fired the Wild into the lead but aside from a few niggly penalties to both teams, that was the only major occurrence in the second period.

This game was very closely matched and could easily have gone either way – and the tension was racked up further around the rink when Billingham equalised 5 minutes into the third period.

There followed another 9 minutes of tense stalemate during which both teams had their chances but were unable to make any headway. Widnes finally edged back into the lead with a goal from Player Coach Richard Haggar on 54 minutes and the atmosphere visibly relaxed among the Wild camp.

Two minutes later, it was 3-1 to Widnes with a goal from Kieran Beach but Billingham still looked dangerous in attack and nothing could be taken for granted with almost 3 minutes still left to play.

The Stars withdrew their netminder for the final 50 seconds in favour of an extra attacking player but this appeared to backfire when Widnes fired in an empty net goal with 47m seconds left on the clock. However, the strike was disallowed due to an infringement and the Wild's Jay Robinson was sent to the box on a checking penalty.

This left Widnes playing 4 against 6 but they managed to hold out for the remaining few seconds and Tom Stubley made sure of the win with a successful empty net strike at 59.37.

Highlighting what a closely fought game it had been, the MVP awards went to the netminders for each side – Thomas Brown for Billingham and Harrison Walker for Widnes – who was icing for the first time since coming back from injury.

The Wild Player of the Month for October was unveiled as Liam Charnock, having been voted in a fans' poll.

The win sees the Wild still in 7th place in the Moralee Division table level on points with Blackburn Hawks, who they have yet to play in the league.

Widnes have played fewer games to date than most of the other teams and positions 4 to 7 in the table are all separated by just 1 point so there is still plenty to play for.

The Wild are without a game next weekend and are next in action on Sunday 28th November when they take on league

Widnes Wild at home to Solway Sharks (Photo by Geoff White)

Sunday 28th November: Moralee Division
YKK Widnes Wild 5 - Solway Sharks 6 (PS)

The YKK sponsored Widnes Wild put in a superb performance against league leaders Solway Sharks, leading for most of the game before ultimately losing out on Penalty Shots, at Planet Ice Widnes on Sunday.

From this performance, you would never guess that 7 league places separated the two teams - and Widnes were never once behind during the whole 65 minutes played.

After a high octane and tense opening, the Wild took the lead in the 9th minute with a powerplay goal from Dani Haid, only to see Solway equalise 4 minutes later.

The score remained 1-1 at the end of the first period but just 70 seconds into the second, Nathan Britton fired Widnes back into the lead.

The advantage was doubled just 2 minutes later as Matty Barlow fired in a powerplay goal and Widnes were bettering the league leaders 3-1.

Solway upped the pressure and forced the Wild into incurring some penalties as they tried to keep the Scottish offence at bay. This resulted in two powerplay goals that saw the scores level again at the end of the second period.

The game was finely balanced on a knife edge and really could have gone either way from this point on. As it turned out, it took until 12 minutes into the third period before the next breakthrough was made – that's a whole 22 minutes since the previous goal – and it fell to Latvian import Vlads Vulkanovs who edged the Wild back in front.

Solway hit back again to make the score 4-4 with just 5 minutes left to play but Vulkanovs found the back of the net once more with just 90 seconds remaining to give the Wild hope of taking their biggest scalp of the season so far.

Unfortunately, those hopes were dashed in the Yellow Camp as the Sharks forced in a last gasp equaliser and sent the game into sudden death overtime.

An extra period of 5 minutes with 3 v 3 on the ice still couldn't separate the two sides so the result had to be decided by Penalty Shots.

Having trailed for most of the game the Sharks finally settled the contest with a 0-2 win on penalties.

That gives Solway 2 points in the league table while Widnes receive 1 point for the draw at the end of regulation time.

The game on Sunday saw the Wild club's annual "Teddy Toss" event where soft toys are collected to be given out to local charities and good causes over the Christmas period. Over 50 gifts were collected, including a number from kind hearted Solway fans who also entered into the spirit.

The Wild are next in action this Sunday 5th December when they take on the Nottingham Lions in the Moralee Division at Planet Ice Widnes – 5.30pm face off.

Wild's Chris Wilcox (#28) receives the MVP award against Nottingham from Terry Gray and Sharon Hanna who had just got married (Photo by Rebecca Clayton)

Sunday 5th December 2021 – Moralee Division
YKK Widnes Wild 7 – Nottingham Lions 2

The YKK sponsored Widnes Wild picked up an important win in the NIHL Moralee Division with a 7-2 victory over league strugglers Nottingham Lions at Planet Ice Widnes on Sunday.

It was a very entertaining game to watch and was, overall, much closer than the final scoreline suggests. The main difference was that Widnes were able to make the most of their chances in front of goal while the Lions were not.

Nottingham actually outshot Widnes in the first period but a great display by netminder Harrison Walker kept the visitors at bay and the Wild took the lead in the 8th minute with a goal from Latvia import Vlads Vulkanovs. Nottingham equalised 3 minutes later but a second Vulkanovs strike in the 17th minute re-established the Widnes lead and the score remained 2-1 at the first period break.

Nottingham equalised again on 26 minutes but Widnes fought back and retook the lead just 80 seconds later with a fine strike from Dani Haid. From that point on, Widnes visibly had the upper hand and a powerplay goal from Mikey Gilbert on 35 minutes handed them a two-goal advantage by the end of the second period.

The third period continued in similar vein with Widnes looking the stronger team but Nottingham stubbornly refusing to throw in the towel. A goal from Jay Robinson on 45 minutes made the score 5-2 to Widnes and a hat-trick goal from Vulkanovs on 48 minutes further extended the advantage.

A goal from Matty Barlow on 52 minutes rounded off the scoring for the game and secured the Wild an important victory as they seek to keep up with the main pack in the Moralee Division league table.

Just one point separates 4 teams in the league standing at present with 4th place Billingham and 5th place Blackburn both on 10 points and then Sheffield and Widnes close behind on 9. The Wild have games in hand over all the other teams in the division so their true position in the table is not really clear at this point.

The after match presentations saw the Most Valuable Player (MVP) awards go to Reaghan Taylor for Nottingham and Chris Wilcox for Widnes and a signed Wild shirt was presented to Junior Academy Chairman Terry Gray and Child Protection Officer Sharon Hanna to celebrate their wedding at the weekend.

Wild celebrations after beating Solway Sharks over 2 legs to reach the Moralee Cup Final (photo by Geoff White)

Moralee Cup Semi Final (2 legs)
Saturday 11th December: Solway Sharks 3 – YKK Widnes Wild 3
Sunday 12th December: YKK Widnes Wild 5 – Solway Sharks 4
(Widnes Win 8-7 on Aggregate)

The YKK sponsored Widnes Wild booked their place in the final of the Moralee Cup with a sensational two legged semi-final victory over highly rated Solway Sharks at the weekend.

They drew 3-3 away in Dumfries on Saturday night before finishing off the job with a highly entertaining and keenly contested 5-4 win at Planet Ice Widnes on Sunday.

The away leg on Saturday was incredibly close and the Wild eventually took the lead with just 90 seconds left in the first period with an acrobatic goal from Latvian import Vlads Vulkanovs.

Solway equalised on 24 minutes but Widnes edged ahead again on 32 with a goal from Joe Greaves. The Sharks pulled level once again just 75 seconds later and the scores remained locked at 2-2 heading into the final period.

This was a superb all round performance from the Wild and while Solway had the upper hand in terms of puck possession and shots on goals for much of the game, it was Widnes who made more of their chances when they came.

That said, a fight in front of Harrison Walker's net between the Wild's Tom Brierley and Solway's Callum Boyd saw both protagonists sent off for the rest of the game and this seemed to lift the Sharks heading into the last 10 minutes.

On the resulting powerplay, Solway took the lead for the first time in the game but a fine effort from Vulkanovs restored parity again and the match finished level, with everything still to play for in the second leg.

In the home game on Sunday, Widnes took the lead after 4 minutes with a fine strike from Vlads Vulkanovs but Solway hit back to lead 1-3 at the first period break.

Widnes pulled a goal back through player coach Richard Haggar just 32 seconds into the second period and, as the Wild piled on the pressure, the visitors began to lose their composure.

A string of penalties for Solway in the second period handed the initiative to Widnes and they made the most of the resulting powerplay opportunities with goals from Vulkanovs on 25 minutes and Joe Greaves on 38 to take the lead.

A further goal from Matty Barlow on 45 minutes put Widnes 5-3 ahead and with one foot in the Cup final but there was more drama still to come.

Solway pulled a goal back with less than two minutes left on the clock and then called a time out to discuss a last minute strategy. They removed their netminder in favour of an extra attacker for the last 75 seconds of the game but were unable to make a breakthrough and Widnes were able to hold and secure their first ever victory over the Sharks.

The 5-4 victory means that Widnes win the tie 8-7 overall on aggregate and now go on to play the winners of the other semi final in a two-legged final, which will take place in the New Year.

The other finalists are yet to be determined as the semi final ties between Solihull Barons and Dundee Comets - which were also due to take place this weekend - were not played due to some problem regarding travel and ice availability so that issue will need to be resolved by the EIHA before details for the Cup final can be confirmed.

The YKK sponsored Widnes Wild have a busy weekend ahead of them as they travel to face Solihull Barons in the league this Saturday 18th December – 5.30pm face off - and are then at home to Sheffield Scimitars on Sunday at Planet Ice Widnes, 5.30pm start.

The Wild are currently playing catch up in the Moralee Division, having played fewer games than most of the other teams. There are currently just three points separating the teams from 3rd to 7th place in the league table and two wins this weekend could potentially see the Wild climb up to 3rd, depending on other results.

Vlads Vulkanovs (#13) beats the Sheffield netminder (Photo by Geoff White)

Saturday 18th December: Solihull Barons 4 – YKK Widnes Wild 5
Sunday 19th December: YKK Widnes Wild 3 – Sheffield Scimitars 2 (OT)

The YKK sponsored Widnes Wild moved up into 3rd place in the Moralee Division table after two wins at the weekend that saw them beat Solihull Barons 4-5 away on Saturday and then secure a dramatic 3-2 overtime win over the Sheffield Scimitars at Planet Ice Widnes on Sunday.

The game on Saturday started well for the Wild as Latvian import Vlads Vulkanovs put them into the lead as early as the 4th minute.

The advantage was doubled two minutes later with a strike from Jay Robinson but Solihull pulled a goal back on 9 minutes to remain in contention.

This game was played at a furious pace throughout it and was very even in terms of puck possession and shots on goal - but it was Widnes who were able to make more of their chances in the opening period.

They went 1-3 ahead with a second goal from Vulkanovs after 11 minutes and that remained the score at the first period break.

The second period continued in a similar vein but with both teams trying to close the play down and not give anything anyway. The next breakthrough came in the 28th minute when Solihull pulled another goal back to narrow the score to 2-3 but Widnes countered and 4 minutes later it was 2-4, courtesy of a goal from Tom Stubley.

The Barons scored again just 34 seconds into the third period and, sensing a possible comeback, noticeably upped their game. They outshot the Wild by 19 to 6 in the final period and the pressure paid off with an equalising goal on 49 minutes.

The final 10 minutes were very tense and the game could have gone either way. Solihull racked up the pressure by calling a time out on 55 minutes but it was Widnes who came away with the points after a hat trick goal from Vulkanovs sealed the win with a goal just 80 seconds from the final buzzer.

Winning away on Saturday might, on paper – at least - have appeared to have been the more difficult of the two tasks for the weekend but Sheffield arrived on Merseyside off the back of a 7-1 win over Blackburn the night before and were also looking to further improve their position in the league standings.

After a very close and evenly matched opening phase, it was the visitors who scored first – on 16 minutes – and the score remained 0-1 at the first period break.

A second goal for Sheffield 4 minutes into the second period set alarm bells ringing in the Yellow Camp but calm was restored just 27 seconds later with a goal from Jay Robinson to open the Widnes account for the night.

Widnes out-shot Sheffield for most of the game but the visiting netminder stubbornly kept them out and the score remained 1-2 after two periods.

The third period saw more Wild attacking and more staunch Sheffield defending, and it wasn't until the 55th minute – an incredible 30 minutes since the previous goal – that Widnes finally equalised with a strike from Latvian import Vlads Vulkanovs.

With no more goals in the remaining 4 ½ minutes, the game went into sudden death overtime and the Wild surged forward once more.

Widnes had by far the more chances on goal but – as the tension mounted around the rink – they were unable to bury the puck in the net.

The clock ticked down and with just 18 seconds left before a penalty shoot out would have to decide the winner, player coach Richard Haggar finally fired the puck home to secure the win for Widnes and round off a successful 4 –point weekend.

Those two wins – coupled with a surprise defeat for Solihull away to bottom club Nottingham, who hadn't won a regular time league game since January 2018, mean that Widnes climb into third place in the Moralee Division table.

They are 9 points behind leading pair Solway Sharks and Whitley Warriors but have games in hand over both teams and plenty more games yet to play in the season.

Wild players Tom Jackson (#84), Mikey Gilbert (#16) & Bez Hughes (#20) somewhat belatedly receive the 2021 North Cup from Eleanor Manson-Sawko, Business Development Manager for Halton Haven Hospice - who are the Wild's chosen charity for the 2021/22 season (Photo by Geoff White)

Widnes Wild 2021 Round Up
By Paul Breeze

The YKK sponsored Widnes Wild finish the calendar year of 2021 in their highest ever league position – 3rd in the NIHL North Moralee Division.

It's a great achievement for player coach Richard Haggar's new look team, especially bearing in mind that, this time last year, most ice rinks were closed across the country and all organised indoor sport was effectively banned due to the coronavirus lockdown measures.

However with the introduction of vaccination programmes, better testing procedures and other enhanced Covid safety measures, the green shoots began to appear in the spring and competitive ice hockey was allowed to return – albeit under very stringent conditions.

The Wild effectively had to move up a division in order to qualify for the English Ice Hockey Associations's new definition of "Elite Status" and had to appoint a designated COVID officer who tested everybody before they were allowed to enter the ice rink.

The games had to be played behind closed doors – with no spectators permitted – and this meant that there was no gate money coming in, which all ice hockey clubs rely on to be able to operate..

In order to offset the huge costs involved in paying for match officials and ice time, a government grant was made available to participating clubs and the Wild appointed former fan favourite Ollie Barron as player coach for a special series of games for the NIHL North Cup.

Teams from the EIHA National Division held their own 4 team competition - as did teams from the NIHL South and the Elite League also ended up playing a 4-team spring series of games.

In order to keep the fans involved and in some cases, generate some revenue, these games were all streamed live via the internet. Some teams in the National Division had already been doing this – and Nottingham Lions had been streaming their NIHL Moralee Division games for a while – but for most other teams this was a new opportunity to make the most of the new technology on offer and to get the message out about their clubs.

Because most of the Elite League and NIHL teams were not playing back in Spring 2021, this allowed the teams that were taking part in these competitions to sign players of a higher calibre who wouldn't normally be available to them and this gave the ice hockey an even more competitive edge than normal.

The NIHL North cup saw the new look Widnes team playing home and away against Sheffield Scimitars, Nottingham Lions and local rivals Blackburn Hawks. They won 4 of their 6 games to finish ahead of Blackburn to top the four-team group and win the trophy.

Ollie Barron stepped down after that series and was replaced by former Hull Jets sniper Richard Haggar who had originally joined the Wild for some match practice while his home rink was closed.

Haggar was then tasked with putting together a new squad to take part in the Three Rivers Tournament which would see Widnes play an 8 match series against Sheffield and Nottingham – meeting each team twice at home and twice away.

This was another highly entertaining competition – once again played "behind closed doors" – and, once again, it saw numerous "guest players" turning out for the three teams involved.

The Wild only managed to win 3 of their 8 games and finished second to Sheffield in the competition, but it was enough to see them qualify for a hastily arranged National Play Off against the top teams from the parallel NIHL South cup competition.

We were now in June and the partial lifting of Covid restrictions meant that a certain number of fans, under strict testing and distancing conditions, were allowed to attend the play off weekend at iceSheffield.

Widnes won their semi final against Slough Jets 5-3 and then beat Sheffield Scimitars 7-4 in the final to be crowned Division 1 National Champions 2021, which was a remarkable achievement for a team that hadn't even been training together 4 months beforehand.

Richard Haggar returned to the Wild as player coach for the new 2021/22 season and was faced with building a squad to take on the likes of Blackburn, Solway, Whitley and Billingham on a regular basis. Here again, Hull's loss was Widnes' gain as, with the Hull Pirates not taking part in the National Division this season, several of their players came to join the ranks of the Wild and add some extra higher division experience.

So, as we look ahead to the rest of the NIHL Moralee Division season in 2022, Widnes could hardly be in a better position.

They are in 3rd place in the league and have played fewer games than any other team. They are, admittedly, 9 points behind second place Whitley Warriors and 11 behind leaders Solway Sharks but they do still have to play both of those teams twice more.

The Wild recently picked up a league point for a regulation time draw away in Dumfries and then beat the Sharks in a two-legged cup semi final so all things are still possible.

They do have a bit of a fixture backlog facing them, however. The league game away at Solihull Barons that was scheduled for Sunday

2nd January has been postponed due to a Covid outbreak in the Wild camp and will have to be rescheduled.

There is also the matter of the two legged Moralee Cup final with home and away games needing to be arranged against Dundee Comets. Indoor sport has been put on hold again in Scotland for the next few weeks and there are only so many match dates available in the calendar so it will be interesting to see how those extra games can be accommodated.

Wild General Manager Wez Spurrett, Coach Mark Gillingham and Player Coach Richard Haggar with the Division 1 National Championship trophy at Sheffield in June 2021 (Photo by Geoff White)

Wild's Dani Haid (#44) out-skates Hawks' Cade King in the OT defeat away at Blackburn (Photo by Trevor Matthews)

Sunday 9th January 2022 – Moralee Division
Blackburn Hawks 5 – YKK Widnes Wild 4 (OT)

The YKK sponsored Widnes Wild narrowly lost out to North West rivals Blackburn Hawks 5-4 in their first game of 2022 which was eventually decided by a dramatic sudden death strike in overtime on Sunday evening.

Widnes actually took the lead in the 8th minute with a goal from Nathan Britton and still led 0-1 at the first period break, however Blackburn upped their game considerably in the second period and mounted a strong recovery.

The Hawks equalised just 3 minutes into the period and then went ahead via a Penalty Shot on 36 minutes after Mikey Gilbert was called for tripping.

The Wild had a much better third period and levelled the score again just 33 seconds from the puck drop with a goal from Tom Stubley.

Blackburn scored again to re-establish a slender lead just 3 minutes afterwards but Widnes player coach Richard Haggar fired in to restore parity once more 2 minutes after that to leave the game finely balanced at 3-3 with 14 minutes left to play.

The game could have gone either way at this point and the next breakthrough fell to Widnes as Haggar scored his second goal of the game to put the Wild back in the lead on 50 minutes. Unfortunately, they weren't able to build further on this and Blackburn drew level again on 52 minutes and the game remained deadlocked at the end of the regulation 60 minutes' playing time.

This sent the game into sudden death overtime to decide a winner and it was the Hawks who emerged triumphant with a "golden goal" at 63.14.

Blackburn receive 2 league points for the Overtime Win and Widnes get 1 point for having drawn at the end of regulation time. This leaves the league table in a fascinating position as just 2 points separate the team in positions 3 to 7. The Wild are currently in 4th place in the Moralee Division table with 14 points – level with 3rd place Solihull and 5th place Sheffield, although they have games in hand over both.

Just behind them are Billingham and Blackburn both on 12 points and, with the Wild due to play the Hawks again this Sunday at Planet Ice Widnes, there will be a lot riding on that game.

*****

The EIHA have confirmed that the two legged final of the Moralee Cup will take place over the weekend of 19th and 20th February 2022.

The YKK Widnes Wild will travel north of the border to face Dundee Comets on Saturday 19th February – 6.30pm face off – with the return leg being played the following day at Planet Ice Widnes – 5.30pm face off.

This means that the Wild's home league game against Blackburn Hawks that had been scheduled for 20th February will now have to be re-arranged.

Mikey Gilbert (#16) and Joe Greaves (#94) put the Blackburn goal under pressure but the Hawks went on to win the game in overtime. (Photo by Geoff White)

Sunday 16th January 2022 – Moralee Division
YKK Widnes Wild 3 – Blackburn Hawks 4

The YKK sponsored Widnes Wild slipped to the bottom half of the Moralee Division table after a frustrating 3-4 home defeat at the hands of north west rivals Blackburn Hawks at Planet Ice Widnes on Sunday.

This was the first home game of the new year for the Wild and was keenly anticipated after the previous meeting between the two teams the week before in East Lancashire ended in a draw and was only won by the Hawks in sudden death overtime.

As is usual with games against Blackburn, the match was played at a furious pace and the sizeable lively crowd contributed to the atmosphere.

The opening period was played out goal-less, which is quite unusual in ice hockey, and the first breakthrough came 70 seconds into the second period when the Hawks opened the scoring.

The Wild had much of the play in this period and outshot the visitors by 2 to 1 but couldn't find a way past the stubborn Blackburn defence. They finally managed a breach with just 16 seconds to go in the period when Liam Charnock fired home to level the score at 1-1.

Blackburn edged ahead again on 43 minutes but Widnes equalised once more 80 seconds later with a goal from former Hawks player Joe Greaves. Blackburn struck again to retake the lead 12 seconds after that and Widnes had to regroup and start again.

The Wild managed to equalise for the third time through a Tom Stubley strike with 10 minutes left on the clock, setting the scene for another dramatic finale.

Unfortunately for the yellow camp, despite chances at both ends, it was Blackburn who scored the next goal – on 57 minutes – and that turned out to be the decider.

The MVP awards went to Matty Barlow for Widnes and former Widnes rec netminder Mike Rogers for Blackburn who, in all fairness, had a very good game and turned away 39 of the 42 shots that he faced.

After the game Widnes netminder Harrison Walker was announced as being Wild Player Of the Month for December, having been voted in a fans' poll on Twitter.

The result leaves 4 teams locked together on 14 points in the Moralee Division table, with Solihull, Sheffield, Blackburn and Widnes occupying third to sixth place, in that order.

With Billingham just points behind on 12 in 7th place, there is still much to play for with the season only halfway through and Widnes having one or more games in hand over all the other teams in the league.

The Wild are next in action this Saturday 22nd January when they travel away to face Sheffield Scimitars in the "steel city" – 7.30pm face off. They are then at home the day after when they take on Nottingham Lions at Planet Ice Widnes, 5.30pm face off.

The Widnes Wild Ladies team are away to Bristol Huskies at the recently opened Planet Ice rink in Bristol on Sunday, 4.45pm face off.

Tempers flare in the home win over Nottingham Lions (Photo by Geoff White)

Sat 22nd January: Sheffield Scimitars 2 – YKK Widnes Wild 1
Sun 23rd January: YKK Widnes Wild 8 – Nottingham Lions 5

The YKK-sponsored Widnes Wild had a mixed weekend losing 2-1 away to Sheffield Scimitars on Saturday and then bouncing back to beat Nottingham Lions 8-5 at home at Planet Ice Widnes on Sunday.

The game on Saturday in Sheffield saw Widnes go behind to a goal in the 13th minute and the deficit then doubled early in the second period.

While not necessarily playing badly – and having a reasonable amount of puck possession and shots on goal themselves - the Wild were clearly not firing on all cylinders and it took until the 49th minute for Latvian import Vlads Vulkanovs to fire in the one and only Widnes goal of the game.

The Wild had a much better start in the home game on Sunday and took the lead after just 2 minutes with a goal from Vlads Vulkanovs.

Dani Haid doubled the advantage on 10 minutes but Nottingham pulled a goal back late in the period to leave the score at 2-1 at the first break.

Widnes continued the second period as they had played the first with plenty of puck possession and outshooting the visitors by a considerable margin. Matty Barlow fired home just two minutes into the period to make the score 3-1 but then, somewhat against the run of play, Nottingham hit two quick fire goals to dramatically equalise.

The Wild's Nathan Britton edged Widnes back into the lead again shortly afterward but there was great controversy right at the end of the period as Nottingham fired the puck into the net just as the buzzer sounded.

After some deliberation, the match officials decided that the goal was valid and the score stood at 4-4 with one period left to play.

(Video evidence has since demonstrated that playing time had expired before the puck had crossed the line and that the goal should, therefore, not have counted. However, in all fairness, the referees did not have access to this facility during the game and had to make a real time decision based on what they had seen in front of them.)

Widnes scored again on 45 minutes through Vulkanovs and Nottingham countered once more two minutes later to level at 5-5. The Wild still had more of the play overall but were having trouble breaking through the stubborn Lions' defence and it began to look if the game might be heading for sudden death overtime.

However, with just over two minutes left in regulation playing time, player coach Richard Haggar fired in an important goal to put Widnes back into the lead.

The Lions called a time out to discuss last ditch tactics and then removed their netminder in favour of an extra attacking player in an attempt to salvage something from the game. That move backfired as Vulkanovs rounded off his hat-trick with a goal in the empty net to make the score 7-5.

Undaunted by the setback, the Lions tried the same tactic again once they had possession on the puck at the Wild end of the ice but the same outcome occurred as Tom Stubley fired home another Empty Net Goal, for a final score of Widnes 8 – Nottingham 5.

Wild's Tom Brierley (#4) Jack Murray #71, Harrison Walker (#32) and Keiron Furlong (#86) combine to thwart a Solway attack (Photo by Geoff White)

Sunday 30th January 2022 – Moralee Division
YKK Widnes Wild 2 – Solway Sharks 5

The YKK sponsored Widnes Wild's recent impressive run of results against the Solway Sharks came to an end with a 2-5 defeat at the hand of the Scottish team at Planet Ice Widnes on Sunday.

Having not lost in normal time to the league leaders in their last 3 meetings, there were hopes that a home win for the Wild would provide a spark for a move up the Moralee Division table but it was not to be.

The game was played at a furious pace throughout and Widnes actually took the lead in the 3rd minute with a powerplay goal from Matty Barlow.

Solway equalised 4 minutes later and despite numerous chances for both teams, the score remained 1-1 at the first break.

The game remained deadlocked for much of the second period – with Solway having more shots on goal but Widnes defending and counter attacking well. The next breakthrough came in the 36th minute and it fell to the home side as Joe Greaves edged the Wild back in front.

However, Solway levelled again just 12 seconds later and the score remained 2-2 after two periods of play.

The Sharks took the lead for the first time in the game with a goal on 42 minutes and the Wild suffered a further setback following an unsavoury incident in the 49th minute.

Joe Greaves made an overly heavy challenge on a Solway player and was handed a 2 minute penalty for cross checking, 2+5 minutes for fighting plus an early shower for being the aggressor. This, unfortunately, left Widnes having to play the next 9 minutes against the league leaders a man short.

In all fairness, they weathered the storm fairly well, going 2-4 down to a powerplay goal on 51 minutes but otherwise seeing off the rest of the penalty without conceding. However all of this time that they were defending, they weren't able to do very much attacking so the Sharks were able to soak up the pressure and save their energy.

A five minute spell back on equal terms at the end was not enough for the Wild to claw themselves back into the game and while they were pushing forward in search of a goal, they were caught out at the back and Solway scored their fifth of the night with just 22 seconds left on the clock.

The win for Solway sees them pull 4 points ahead of second place Whitley Warriors at the top of the Moralee Division table. Solihull Barons are third after a win away to Billingham Stars with 18 points and Widnes and Sheffield are next both on 16 points, although the Wild have games in hand over the Scimitars and the top two.

The Wild are next in action this Sunday 6th February when they travel away to face Nottingham Lions – 5.00pm face off. They are then at home the Sunday after, 13th February, when they take on Solihull Barons at Planet Ice Widnes, 5.30pm face off.

The Widnes Wild Ladies team are at home to Chelmsford Cobras on Sunday 6th February at Planet Ice Widnes, 4.15pm face off.

Sunday 6th February 2022 – Moralee Division
Nottingham Lions 3 - YKK Widnes Wild 4

The YKK sponsored Widnes Wild came away from the Lace City with a narrow 3-4 win over Nottingham Lions on Sunday.

Widnes took the lead in the 6th minute with a goal from Jay Robinson and doubled the advantage on 15 minutes with a strike from Matty Barlow.

Nottingham struck back with a goal of their own just 40 seconds later but the 2-goal cushion was restored with just 3 seconds left in the period with a goal from the Wild's Latvian import Vlads Vulkanovs.

A second goal from Vulcanovs 4 minutes from the restart put the Wild 1-4 up and they looked to be cruising, but despite numerous chances for both teams, that was to be the only goal of the second period.

The Wild eased off and defended their lead in the third period and, as a result Nottingham had a far bigger proportion of the play. They dragged a goal back on 45 minutes and then narrowed the defecit to just one goal with a powerplay strike 7 minutes later.

Widnes weathered this late storm, however, and held on to win the game 3-4 – with netminder Evan Coles putting in a super performance to stop 47 of the 50 shots fired at him, resulting in an overall Save Percentage of 94.00% over the 60 minutes.

The result sees the Wild remain in 5th place in the Moralee Division table, 2 points clear of Billingham and 2 behind 4th place Sheffield both of whom they have games in hand over.

Vlads Vulkanovs remains the Moralee Division's top goal scorer with 20 strikes in 15 league games, level with Solihull's Thomas Soar.

The Wild are back in action this Sunday 13th February when they take on Solihull Barons at Planet Ice Widnes, 5.30pm face off.

The weekend after that they have the two legged final of the highly prestigious Moralee Cup where they play Dundee Comets home and away. The first leg is away in Dundee on Saturday 19th February, face off 7.30 pm, and the return leg is the next day at Planet Ice Widnes, 5.30pm start.

Sunday 13th February – Moralee Division
YKK Widnes Wild 6 – Solihull Barons 4

The YKK sponsored Widnes Wild moved up to 4th place in the Moralee Division table with a hard fought 6-4 win over Solihull Barons at Planet Ice Widnes on Sunday.

The game was very evenly matched throughout – between two teams who are neck and neck in terms of league placings - and was, overall, a very good advert for NIHL ice hockey.

Widnes took the lead on 7 minutes with a goal from Josh Reynolds, who was making his first appearance for the Wild, and went further ahead on 15 with a strike from Latvian import Vlads Vulcanovs.

Solihull hit back 90 seconds later to halve the deficit but the score remained 2-1 to Widnes at the first period break.

Goals were exchanged in the second period with two for each side – Vulkanovs and player coach Richard Haggar finding the net for Widnes – and the game remained finely balanced at 4-3 with one period left to play.

Matty Barlow edged the Wild further ahead on 43 minutes and a short handed hat-trick goal for Vulkanovs 7 minutes later looked to have given Widnes a winning lead.

However, Solihull pulled a goal back on 52 minutes and the Wild had a nervy last few minutes to hang on before securing the win.

The win sees the Wild move to within 1 point of the third place Barons with a game in hand and two meetings still to come between the two sides.

As we progress in the second half of the season all of these games take on an extra importance as the final league positions will decide who plays who in the playoffs, with the higher finishing teams getting an easier draw in the quarter finals.

At the end of the game, Tom Stubley was unveiled as the Wild Player of the Month for January, having been selected by fans via an online Twitter poll.

COUNTDOWN TO THE MORALEE CUP FINAL

Former Wild player and coach Richard Charles hails from Dundee (Photo by Geoff White)

The YKK sponsored Widnes Wild have a hugely important weekend ahead of them as they take on the Dundee Comets in a two legged final to decide who will win the first major trophy of the season – the highly prestigious Moralee Cup.

They make a first ever trip to Dundee for the away leg on Saturday and then play the second leg at Planet Ice Widnes on Sunday, 5.30pm face off.

This keenly anticipated final is easily the biggest game to be staged at Planet Ice Widnes since the Laidler Play Off final in April 2019 and could reasonably be viewed as the biggest ever game to date.

Their opposition in the two-legged final – Dundee Comets – are pretty much an unknown quantity as they play in the Scottish National League. They have won the SNL league title three times – most recently in the 2017/18 season when they also won the Play Off title. They beat Whitley and Billingham home and away in their Moralee Cup qualifying group but lost both games against Solway Sharks, finishing second overall out of the four teams, the same as Widnes did in their group.

The Comets play in the 2000-seater Dundee Arena – which is also home to the Dundee Stars Elite League team and the Dundee Tigers SNL side – and the Tayside club has a long tradition of producing successful teams and developing home grown talent.

Former Wild player and coach Richard Charles originates from Dundee and played junior and senior hockey there for many years. Commenting on the set up there, he said:

"The current ice rink was built after I left Dundee so I never got to play officially on the pad, but have been on it many times skating and scrimmaged there a few times. It's a great facility – nice surface, good facilities and a reasonable amount of spectator seating. I've attended a few Stars games many years ago and there was a great atmosphere."

"John Dolan is a key player to keep an eye on in the Dundee team. He has played over 350 games at Elite League level for the Dundee Stars and Fife Flyers and, before that some 70 games in the British National League, with over 300 career goals to his name."

The away leg of the Cup Final is to be played in Dundee on Saturday 19th February – 7.30pm face off – and the home leg is on the day after, Sunday 20th February, at Planet Ice Widnes starting at 5.30pm.

Admission for the home game is £11 for adults and £6 for children and tickets can be booked in advance via the online booking system.

Wild captain Tom Jackson receives the Moralee Cup trophy from EIHA Director Barrie Archer (Photo by Geoff White)

Wild Win Moralee Cup Final!

Saturday 19th February: Dundee Comets 3 – YKK Widnes Wild 3
Sunday 20th February: YKK Widnes Wild 4 – Dundee Comets 3
(Widnes Win 7-6 on Aggregate)

The YKK sponsored Widnes Wild won the first major trophy of the Moralee Division season with a two legged victory over the Dundee Comets in the league cup final over the weekend. They drew 3-3 away in Scotland on Saturday night before completing the job with a 4-3 win in front of a capacity crowd at Planet Ice Widnes on Sunday.

The first leg was played at the impressive 2000 seater Dundee Arena and Widnes got off to a dream start with a goal from Dani Haid just 90 seconds into the game.

Dundee equalised three minutes later and then edged ahead three minutes after that but the lead lasted only 30 seconds before Vlads Vulcanovs fired in a superb individual goal to put Widnes back on level pegging.

The Wild scored again on 15 minutes through Matty Barlow and the score remained at 2-3 at the first period break.

There was an unsavoury incident on 28 minutes when the Wild's Joe Wyatt made a clumsy and over-heavy challenge on a Dundee attacker and, as a result, was then pummelled to the ground by an irate Comet. Both players received match penalties for their efforts and played no further part in the game.

This game was very closely matched overall and highly entertaining to watch but the only other goal came in the 39th minute when Dundee fired in an equaliser to leave the Cup Final tie finely balanced at 3-3 ready for the return leg in Widnes the following day.

The home leg on Sunday was played in front of a full house at the Planet Ice rink and the Wild got off to an even better start than the previous game with a goal from Tom Stubley after just 17 seconds.

Dundee hit back with a short handed goal on 5 minutes but despite further chances for both teams, the game remained deadlocked at 1-1 on the night - and 4-4 on aggregate - at the first period break.

Widnes were on top for much of this game and outshot the Comets by 51 to 32 over the entire 60 minutes. Fortunes swung firmly in the Wild's favour in the second period when a series of niggly penalties left the visitors short handed and Widnes re-took the lead with a powerplay goal from player coach Richard Haggar on 25 minutes.

The lead was extended with another powerplay goal - from Dani Haid - 3 minutes later and Widnes led the home leg 3-1 at the half way stage. Dundee pulled a goal back on 32 minutes and the rest of the period played out goalless to leave the game very much on a knife edge heading into the final period.

Following a tense phase after the restart Liam Charnock restored the two-goal advantage for Widnes with a goal on 49 minutes to hand them a 4-2 lead. But Dundee were by no means not out of it and they scored again 4 minutes later to set up a barnstorming finale to this thrilling Cup Final.

The remaining time clicked down agonisingly slowly for the Widnes players and fans and Dundee withdrew their netminder for the last 90 seconds in favour of an extra attacker in an attempt to force a last-ditch equaliser.

The Wild defence held strong however and the score at the final buzzer – 4-3 on the night and 7-6 on aggregate - signified a fantastic achievement for Richard Haggar's squad in their debut season in the Moralee Division.

The Moralee Cup trophy was presented by EIHA Director Barrie Archer to Widnes Captain Tom Jackson and the MVP awards went to Dundee Captain Billy Baxter and Wild's Liam Charnock.

Following on from the weekend's excitement, Wild General Manager Wez Spurrett said:

"What an incredible weekend, on and off the ice. I want to thank everyone that made the journey up to Dundee on Saturday to support the team. It was already a tough distance but with the added weather complications the team were incredibly appreciative of the support that greeted us, and the noise they created."

"The crowd and the atmosphere on Sunday was something I haven't experienced before - just electric. We cannot put into words just how much it helped the team when we needed it the most."

"I couldn't be prouder of the team. From the drop of the puck on Saturday until the final buzzer on Sunday they gave it everything. And you could see just how much they wanted it by how many threw their bodies in the way of so many shots in the dying minutes. We couldn't have asked any more from them and they truly deserve the rewards this weekend."

"Massive congratulations have to go to Dundee Comets too, for making the final and providing a memorable weekend of hockey. It's easy to forget they were only one shot away from taking the final into overtime and beyond. So great work from their team and coaching staff."

"We will, of course, enjoy this moment, but we will be back to work at training this week to finish this season strongly."

The YKK sponsored Widnes Wild return to league action this Sunday 27th February when they take on second place team Whitley Warriors at Planet Ice Widnes – 5.30pm face off.

Wild player coach Richard Haggar (#19) and Dani Haid (#44) celebrate Haggar's second period goal that made the score on the night 2-1 to Widnes in the Moralee Cup Final (Photo by Geoff White)

Wild players, team staff and fans celebrate the Moralee Cup win
(Photo by Geoff White)

Wild netminder Harrison Walker (#32) makes a save in the penalty shootout against Whitley Warriors (Photo by Geoff White)

Sunday 27th February 2022 – Moralee Division
Widnes Wild 3 – Whitley Warriors 4 (PS)

The YKK sponsored Widnes Wild picked up a sensational point in a battling encounter with the Whitley Warriors before eventually losing out on penalty shots at Planet Ice Widnes on Sunday.

After a tense opening, Whitley took the lead on 11 minutes and edged further ahead just 60 seconds later. Widnes pulled a goal back through Liam Charnock just 60 seconds after that and the score remained 1-2 at the first period break.

The Warriors scored again on 28 minutes to lead 1-3 and looked to be well on top at this point. However the Wild team did not let their heads drop and with the score still standing at 1-3 after two periods, still looked to be in with a chance.

The third period was much better for Widnes as they finally managed to match the visitors in terms of puck possession and shots on goal.

Latvian import Vlads Vulcanovs pulled a goal back for the Wild on 48 minutes – and the fightback was on!

On 55 minutes, Matty Barlow fired in the equaliser, setting a up barnstorming finale in a match that could now easily go either way.

The five remaining minutes were played out goal-less, however, as were the resulting 5 minutes of sudden death over time. This meant that the game had to be decided by a penalty shoot out, which – unfortunately for Widnes - went in favour of the visitors.

However the Wild receive a league point for drawing the match at the end of regulation time, and that means that they have now taken points off all of the teams in the Moralee Division this season.

There are three teams currently locked on 21 points in the league table – Sheffield Scimitars, Solihull Barons and Widnes – and the Wild have games in hand over the others.

Widnes now have three away games in a row – away to Solihull this Saturday, Whitley on Sunday and then Solway Sharks on Saturday 12th March. They are next at home on Sunday 13th March when they take on the Solihull Barons at Planet Ice Widnes – 5.30pm face off.

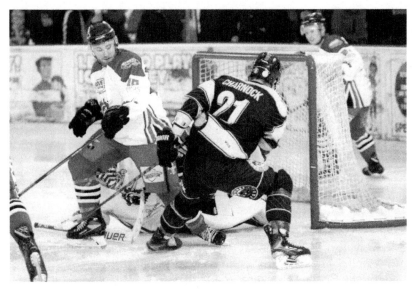

Widnes Wild away at Solihull Barons (Photo by Keith & Jenny Davies)

Saturday 5th March: Solihull Barons 2 – YKK Widnes Wild 6
Sunday 6th March: Whitley Warriors 8 – YKK Widnes Wild 2

The YKK sponsored Widnes Wild moved up into 3rd place in the Moralee Division table after a mixed weekend that saw them lose 8-2 away to Whitley Warriors on Sunday but win 2-6 in the critical "4 pointer" encounter against Solihull Barons on Saturday.

The game on Saturday away at Solihull was a very tight knit affair – as you'd expect from two teams locked on the same number of points in the league table.

The Barons took the lead on 9 minutes but Widnes equalised through Bez Hughes 4 minutes later and the score remained 1-1 at the first period break.

The game remained deadlocked with no goals in the second period until Liam Charnock fired in a short handed strike on 32 minutes to give Widnes the lead for the first time. Both teams had their chances but that was the only breakthrough of the period and the score stood at a tantalisingly close 1-2 to the Wild after 40 minutes of play.

Widnes came out firing on all cylinders for the third period and edged further ahead with a second goal from Charnock just 59 seconds from the restart. Three more goals followed – from Hughes and Vlads Vulkanovs and a powerplay strike from player coach Richard Haggar made the score 1-6 with 8 minutes left on the clock.

A second goal for Solihull on 57 minutes came too late in the game to inspire a late comeback and the Wild held strong for the remaining time to record an important 2-6 victory.

The game away in the North East on Sunday was always going to be a much sterner test and Widnes were up against it right from the start. Whitley took the lead on 5 minutes and led 1-0 at the first period break.

The home side were clearly on top for much of the game and outshot Widnes by 56 to 27 over the course of the full 60 minutes. Three more goals in the early part of the second period handed them a 4-0 lead by the time Vlads Vulcanovs finally found the back of the net for the Wild on 33 minutes.

A second Widnes goal followed just 90 seconds later from Dani Haid but any hopes of a fightback in the black and yellow camp were dashed by another Warriors strike just 60 seconds after that.

A short handed goal for the hosts with less than a minute to play in the period made the score 6-2 to Whitley, putting them firmly in the driving seat with 20 minutes left to play.

Two further goals followed in the third period – which the Wild had no answer to - and Whitley were able to notch up their 4th win out of four over Widnes for the league season.

The weekend results leave the Moralee Division league table as close as ever with three teams still in contention for a third place finish. Widnes and Solihull have 23 points and Sheffield Scimitars have 22.

Leaders Solway Sharks (41 points) and second place Whitley (36) have a clear lead at the top and are unlikely to be caught but the battle for third place is important as the quarter final pairings for the end of season play offs are decided by final league positions.

Wild's Bez Hughes (#20) and Jay Robinson (#90) in action at Solway.
(Photo by Helen Hobbins Photography)

Saturday 12th March: Solway Sharks 9 – YKK Widnes Wild 3
Sunday 13th March: YKK Widnes Wild 8 – Solihull Barons 4

The YKK sponsored Widnes Wild consolidated their third place position in the Moralee Division table with a weekend that saw a 9-3 defeat away at league leaders Solway Sharks on Saturday and then an 8-4 win over fellow play-off hopefuls Solihull Barons at Planet Ice Widnes on Sunday.

The loss away in Scotland to the runaway "champions elect" was always on the cards but the game against Solihull was a real "4 pointer" and the Wild now sit clear of the Barons on points, and with a game in hand heading into the final furlong of the league season.

In the game at Solway on Saturday, the first period started off pretty even with the Sharks taking the lead on 7 minutes and Liam Charnock equalising for the Wild just 90 seconds later.

Solway edged ahead again with a delayed penalty goal on a hooking call on 13 minutes and went on to lead 3-1 at the first period break.

A fourth goal for the Sharks 5 minutes from the restart was cancelled out by a Tom Stubley goal but any hopes of a Widnes fightback were dashed when Joe Greaves got into a fight and was ejected from the game for kneeing. Solway scored on the resulting powerplay and a further goal late in the period saw them lead 6-2 after 40 minutes of play.

Three unanswered Sharks goals early in the third period put the game well and truly out of Widnes' reach and a Matty Barlow strike with 10 minutes left to play rounded off the action for the night.

The home game on Sunday saw Solihull take the lead after 3 minutes and it took until the 15th minute for the Wild's Latvian import Vlads Vulkanovs to fire in the equaliser.

Solihull hit back with two quick goals late in the period slightly against the run of play and led 1-3 at the first break.

Three straight goals in the second period – two from Player / Coach Richard Haggar and one from Mikey Gilbert - edged Widnes into the lead for the first time by the half way point of the contest – but Solihull kept battling away and tied the game at 4-4 with one period left to play.

The Wild upped their game considerably in the last period and threw the proverbial kitchen sink at the Barons – outshooting them by 24 to 10 in the final 20 minutes.

The pressure paid off as three more goals from Vulkanovs (to give him an impressive 4 in the game) and one from Dani Haid saw Widnes coast to an 8-4 victory, which gave them a clean sweep over Solihull in the 4 league meetings this season and also handed them the initiative in the battle for the end of season play off places.

Vulkanovs' four-goal haul means that he remains the top goal scorer in the Moralee Division for the season so far with 30 strikes in 19 games

Solway's Peter Gapa and Nottingham's Zachary Yokoyama are joint second with 27 goals each. Gapa leads the scoring standings in terms of overall points with 52, while the Wild's Richard Haggar has the highest number of assists and currently sits in third in the list with 12+33=45.

The Wild are away in East Lancashire next Sunday 20th March when they take on North West rivals Blackburn Hawks – 6pm face off. They then have two home games the following weekend – against Blackburn on Saturday 26th March and Billingham on Sunday 27th March.

A special "double header" ticket offer has been made available for fans to be able to watch both home games that weekend at a reduced price. The double header weekend ticket will cost £17.00 for adults and £10.00 for children and will cover both games. This represents a saving of £5 on the normal cost of two games for adults and £2 for children.

The special "Weekend" tickets must be purchased in advance, either in person from the Box Office at Planet Ice Widnes or via the online booking system. More information can be found on the Wild club website at www.widneswild.co.uk.

WILD SUPPORT FOR UKRAINE

The Widnes Wild club showed their support for the Ukraine at their home game against Solihull Barons on Sunday by illuminating the exterior of the Planet Ice rink in the blue and yellow colours of the Ukrainian flag and by playing the Ukrainian national anthem before the game.

An ice hockey stick signed by all the players was raffled off and a total of £327 was raised to be donated to the Red Cross appeal for the embattled nation.

In a separate non- club related venture, former Wild team manager Jon Anderson is driving a one-man aid convoy with a van full of donated medical supplies, blankets and food across to the Polish / Ukrainian border where the goods will be distributed via local aid organisations.

Rough stuff at Blackburn after 52 minutes as Widnes go on to pick up their first league win of the season over the Hawks (Photo by Trevor Matthews)

Sunday 20th March – Moralee Division:
Blackburn Hawks 3 – YKK Widnes Wild 8

The YKK sponsored Widnes Wild gave their hopes of a third place finish in the Moralee Division table a mighty boost with a 3-8 victory over north west rivals Blackburn Hawks on Sunday.

Despite being outshot by some 2 to 1 over the course of the game, it was Blackburn who took the lead on 5 minutes and then went on to take a 2-0 advantage into the first period break.

Widnes moved up a gear in the second period and a powerplay goal from Latvian import Vlads Vulcanovs just 19 seconds from the restart halved the deficit.

A goal from Tom Stubley on 24 minutes levelled the score but Blackburn edged back into the lead 3 minutes later.

Widnes equalised again through Player Coach Richard Haggar on 29 minutes and then went ahead for the first time in the game courtesy of a Matty Barlow strike with 2 minutes left in the period.

Three unanswered goals early in the third period – from Bez Hughes, Vulkanovs and Dani Haid - handed Widnes a commanding 3-7 lead and things began to get a bit niggly as the Hawks saw the game slipping away from them.

A series of fights broke out on 52 minutes that saw two players from each team banished to the penalty box and, in the ensuing powerplay, Richard Haggar scored his second Widnes goal of the night to round off the scoring for the game.

With just over a minute left in the game Wild's Joe Greaves got involved in an altercation with former Widnes player Lee Pollitt and at the final buzzer Lee Kemp got involved with another former Wild player Matt Wainwright and got handed a match penalty for his efforts.

Solway Sharks were confirmed as Moralee Division champions at the weekend without even having to step onto the ice after the other various results around the league went in their favour.

Two defeats for second place Whitley Warriors mean they can no longer catch the Sharks at the top of the table but they are safe as runners up as they have a 12 point advantage over the Wild with just 4 games left to play in the regular season.

The situation is much closer as you look further down the table, however, and just 3 points separate places 3 to 6 with Widnes, Solihull, Sheffield and Billingham all still in the hunt for third spot.

Mid season two-way signing Josh Reynolds (#23) receives the MVP award after the Blackburn game from former Wild player Chris Preston. Club Chairman Matt Lloyd also seems pleased. (Photo by Geoff White)

Saturday 26th March 2022 – Moralee Division:
YKK Widnes Wild 5 – Blackburn Hawks 2

The YKK sponsored Widnes Wild edged closer to securing a third place finish with a 5-2 win at home to Blackburn Hawks at Planet Ice Widnes on Saturday in game that saw few of the dramas that had clouded previous encounters between the two sides.

Widnes opened the scoring after just 22 seconds with a goal from Latvian import Vlads Vulcanovs and 4 minutes later the score was 2-0 courtesy of Mikey Gilbert.

The Wild were very much on top in this first period – outshooting the visitors by an incredible 30 to 12 – and they were further rewarded with a 3rd goal on 11 minutes – a powerplay effort from the stick of Vulcanovs again.

Blackburn eventually found the back of the net themselves in the 14th minute on a delayed penalty call against Joe Greaves for interference but the score remained healthy looking 3-1 to Widnes at the first period break.

The second period saw a great improvement for the Hawks in terms of puck possession and shots on goal but they still had great difficulty finding a way past Widnes netminder Harrison Walker. In fact Widnes scored again – on 28 minutes through Liam Charnock – to further extend the advantage, before Blackburn hit back 30 seconds later to score what would turn out to be their only other goal of the game.

The remainder of the game was rather subdued as the Wild elected to sit back to protect their lead and save their energy for the next day's home game against Billingham.

The scoring for the evening was eventually rounded off in the 53rd minute with Liam Charnock's second goal of the game – and the result means that Widnes can claim North West bragging rights over the Hawks for the season - at least by virtue of "goals scored" in the 6 games between the two teams (33 –20), which saw 3 wins for each side.

Liam Charnock (#21) scored 2+2 in the win over Blackburn Hawks
(Photo by Geoff White)

*Matty Barlow (#89) celebrates a Wild goal against Billingham on Sunday
(Photo by Geoff White)*

Sunday 27th March 2022 – Moralee Division
YKK Widnes Wild 5 – Billingham Stars 2

The YKK sponsored Widnes Wild made sure of finishing in third place in the Moralee Division league table with a four point weekend that saw them notch up home wins over Blackburn Hawks and Billingham Stars.

This represents a superb achievement for a team who are playing their first ever season in this higher division as it means they will finish above several other long established teams.

In the game on Saturday, the Wild swept past a numerically deficient Blackburn side with few of the dramas that had clouded previous encounters between the two sides.

The game on Sunday against Billingham Stars was remarkable for several different reasons. As you would expect, it was highly entertaining with both teams still in the race for important finishing positions in the Moralee Division table but, with it being such a finely balanced opening to the game, neither team was able to make an early breakthrough.

That means that it was goal-less at the end of the first period and, quite unusually for a senior men's NIHL game, there were no penalties handed out either.

The first goal – when it did come – fell to the visitors, who eventually took the lead in the 27th minute. Widnes equalised 6 minutes later with a goal from Mikey Gilbert but Billingham edged back into the lead with 3 minutes to go in the period and held on to lead 1-2 at the second break.

Despite the scoreline at this stage, Widnes were well on top throughout this game in terms of puck possession and shots on goal and their superiority finally began to pay off in the third period.

Tom Stubley fired in the equalising goal on 44 minutes and then Nathan Britton put the Wild into the lead for the first time in the game 4 minutes later.

A goal from Joe Greaves on 55 minutes put a bit of daylight between the two teams and Latvian import Vlads Vulcanovs made sure of the win with his 35th league goal of the season with just over 2 minutes left in the game.

The whole game was played without a single penalty being awarded which is a very rare occurrence in competitive men's ice hockey.

The two wins for Widnes over the weekend – along with defeats for Solihull and Sheffield - mean that the Wild can not be overtaken by the chasing pack and are guaranteed to finish in third place in the Moralee Division, in their first ever season playing at that level.

They have two more games in their regular season schedule before the play off quarter finals, which take place over the Easter weekend.

These are:

Sunday 3rd April: away @ Billingham Stars (5.30pm face off)
Sunday 10th April: home v Sheffield Scimitars (5.30pm face off)

Mikey Gilbert (#16) receives a special presentation for having passed 100 games with the Wild from Barry Sprakes and Toni Gilbert (Photo by Geoff White)

The YKK sponsored Widnes Wild were pleased to make a special award to fan favourite Mikey Gilbert after the home game against Billingham on Sunday to recognise his having passed 100 games with the club.

Gilbert joined the Wild from Altrincham Aces back in the summer of 2017 and has now notched up 127 games in Widnes colours, scoring 69 goals, 97 assists and accumulating 141 PIM.

He was presented with a Wild shirt signed by all the players with his name and "100" printed on the back.

Sunday 3rd April 2022 – Moralee Division:
Billingham Stars 2 – YKK Widnes Wild 4

The YKK sponsored Widnes Wild rounded off a clean sweep of wins for the season over the Billingham Stars with a 2-4 victory away in the North East on Sunday.

It was their 4th win in 4 starts against the Teesside team this season and, along with similar 100% records against the Solihull Barons and Nottingham Lions, represents a superb achievement for a team who are playing their first ever season in this higher Moralee Division.

Billingham took the lead in the 5th minute of the game – which was very closely contested throughout – but Widnes equalised 4 minutes later with a strike from top goal scorer Vlads Vulcanovs.

The second period saw Billingham take the lead again 25 minutes but, once again, Widnes drew level - with another Vulcanovs goal three minutes later.

The Wild took the lead for the first time in the game with a goal from player/coach Richard Haggar on 33 minutes and the score remained at 2-3 at the second break.

Billingham gave a very good account of themselves throughout the game and out-shot the Wild by some margin but were unable to make the most of their chances. Instead, Widnes went on to extend the lead with a 4th goal on 54 minutes from Tom Stubley and they held on to notch up another important victory.

Although there are still games left to be played in the Moralee Division's regular season, the results over the weekend mean that the pairings for the Play Off Quarter Finals are all confirmed. The quarter finals will be played over two legs, home and away, on the weekend of 16th & 17th April and will feature:

Solway Sharks v Nottingham Lions, Whitley Warriors v Blackburn Hawks, Widnes Wild v Billingham Stars and Sheffield Scimitars v Solihull Barons.

The winners of each tie will progress to the Moralee Play Off weekend, which will be staged at Planet Ice Leeds the following weekend.

Wild netminder Evan Coles (#39) and Captain Tom Jackson (#84) foil a Sheffield attack. (Photo by Geoff White)

Sunday 10th April 2022 – Moralee Division:
YKK Widnes Wild 9 – Sheffield Scimitars 3

The YKK sponsored Widnes Wild rounded off their regular Moralee Division campaign with a comprehensive 9-3 win over Sheffield Scimitars at Planet Ice Widnes on Sunday.

The game started well for Widnes with Player Coach Richard Haggar opening the scoring on 4 minutes and then doubling the advantage 5 minutes later.

Sheffield – who had arrived on Merseyside with a "2 and 1" record against the Wild so far for the season - gave as good as they got in the first period but were unable to breach the Widnes defences and the score remained 2-0 at the first break.

A straight hat-trick goal for Haggar just 16 seconds into the second period edged Widnes further ahead and then goals from Nathan Britton and Dani Haid saw the Wild leading 5-0 at the mid point in the game.

With half an eye on next weekend's play off quarterfinals, Widnes eased off the gas after this and Sheffield were able to up their own part in the proceedings.

They scored two goals of their own in the latter stages of the second period to bring the score back to 5-2 and then a third strike 3 minutes into the final period narrowed the deficit to just 2 goals.

However Mikey Gilbert fired in a 6th goal for Widnes just 90 seconds later to steady the ship and Widnes were back on top again.

Further goals followed from Vlads Vulkanovs, Liam Charnock and Dani Haid and the Wild finished off their debut season in the Moralee Division with a highly creditable 9-3 win.

After the game, Matty Barlow was named Wild Player of the Month for March.

The full Moralee Division schedule for the season was completed at the weekend as all teams played their final outstanding games.

The Wild finish up in 3rd place in the league table with 18 wins from their 28 matches, which is an impressive achievement for a team playing up in this higher league for the first time.

The Wild huddle for the last game of the regular league season
(Photo by Geoff White)

The Wild line up at the Billingham Forum for the away leg of the Play Off Quarter Final. (Photo by Linda Crabtree)

Moralee Play Off Quarter Final
Saturday 16th April: Billingham Stars 8 – YKK Widnes Wild 1
Sunday 17th April: YKK Widnes Wild 3 – Billingham Stars 2

The YKK sponsored Widnes Wild rounded off their highly successful first season up in the Moralee Division with a 3-2 win over Billingham Stars at Planet Ice Widnes on Sunday.

Unfortunately, this victory was not enough to propel them into the Play Off Final weekend – to be held at Leeds next week - as they lost the away leg of this quarter final encounter 8-1 away in the North East on Saturday and therefore crashed out of the knockout round 10-4 on aggregate.

In the away game in Billingham on Saturday, things started badly for the Wild and just got worse over the course of the match.

The Stars opened the scoring after 5 minutes and were 2-0 up by the first break. In all fairness, Widnes had an equal share of puck possession and shots on goal but were unable to make them count.

Two further goals from Billingham at the start of the second period - within just 9 seconds of each other – really put the Wild on the back foot and a 5th goal at the midway point of the game left Widnes with a metaphorical mountain to climb in the third period.

The Wild threw the kitchen sink at the Stars goal in the final period outshooting the hosts by a massive 21 to 8 but it was Billingham, again, who scored the next goal on 43 minutes to extend the lead to 6-0.

The Widnes efforts were finally rewarded with a strike from player coach Richard Haggar but any hopes of a late comeback were thwarted by more impressive play by the home defence. To make matters worse, the Wild were then caught out at the back while pushing forward to try and reduce the deficit in advance of the home leg and conceded two more goals late in the game.

The 8-1 defeat was the Wild's first loss after 6 straight wins and was their lowest goal haul since a 2-1 defeat away at Sheffield back in January. It also represented the first time in 5 starts that Billingham had recorded a win over Widnes this season.

The home game on Sunday was especially tense – particularly considering what was at stake – and after a nervy opening from both sides, the first period ended goal-less.

Billingham took the lead with a powerplay goal on 26 minutes to lead 9-1 on aggregate but Bez Hughes equalised for the Wild 3minutes later and Latvian import Vlads Vulcanovs edged Widnes in front three minutes after that. While pushing forward to try and extend the lead, the Widnes were caught out by a short handed strike on 35 minutes and that left the score standing at a finely balanced 2-2 at the second period break.

A combination of a later than usual than usual start due to the Laidler Play Off final having been played at the rink earlier in the day and the huge task of trying to overturn a large deficit from the first leg left had led to a rather subdued atmosphere around the rink but the Wild team and fans – while faced with the almost impossible task of scoring 8 unanswered goals in the final period - gave it one last push to finish off the season with style.

These efforts were rewarded when Liam Charnock fired the puck into the net on 52 minutes to retake the lead and Widnes were able to hold on for the 3-2 win.

Thanks From The Widnes Wild GM, Wez Spurrett.

To say that this last weekend didn't go to plan would be an understatement. However following Saturday's result, the team once again showed their character and put on a gutsy performance to dig deep and finish the season with a win. I can tell you from being in the dressing room on Sunday every team chat had one theme, to give it their all for the fans one last time. This just epitomises the teams ethos and ethics, that brings me an immense amount of pride to look at the team we have built this season.

Although this is not the way we wanted our season to end, a huge congratulations must be given to the Billingham Stars and their coaching team for a hard fought playoff weekend of hockey, which after their game plan execution at home on Saturday we were unable to overcome. Another reminder of just how close the league is, where everyone proved that any team can beat anyone on their day.

Now that the dust has settled on this weekend's results, we have the chance to reflect on the past 8 months that this season has brought us all.

This season personally has been a learning curve to say the least. I still remain grateful for the faith Chairman Matt Lloyd had to give me the opportunity to run the team. As it was my first season in a GM role for a hockey team, there was much to learn along the way. Luckily we had great leadership within the team that were able to steer both me and Rich back on the right tracks if we ever started veering off.

Not only was it just a new GM in the club, there was a new head coach as well a number of fresh players. Which, of course, came with their own challenges. Challenges that I hope you can all agree with me, have been overcome with excellent results.

Rich has done an incredible job with the team, ending the season in 3rd place in the league and cup champions, all within his first season as a head coach. I cannot wait to see what he can do next season and beyond.

He has put so much effort in behind the scenes to make himself the best coach he can be, and so that the team can be the best prepared team on the ice, which has clearly shown in many of the results this year.

Thank you to Rich for all of his efforts this season, we look forward to seeing more of the same in the coming seasons.

With a new dressing room there are always uncertainties around how they will all click, and what kind of atmosphere it will be. But the team gelled together straight away from the start, making mine and Rich's job much easier. Throughout the season the team has regularly pulled each other through games, showing just how much character is in that room. Even when results haven't gone our way, the team continued to get behind each other and push to rectify it in the next game.

There wasn't a single member of that team that didn't give it their all, every single shift or every game - which is all you can ask of your players.

So thank you to every player that gave it their all for the Wild this season. It has been a pleasure to call you Widnes Wild players.

Behind the players there is a room full of people that make each game happen, on and off the ice.

I would really like to thank Bob Bramah and his amazing team of students from the University of Salford that have quite literally been patching the team up and keeping them on the ice every week. Your work has been invaluable.

Thank you to our off ice team with Mark Gillingham coming back to the coaching team this year, offering us priceless advice and ideas that have helped us to achieve so many great things this year.

Thanks to Louis Rosslyn for a great job as our equipment manager this season, making sure the players had everything they needed to be able to perform.

And of course to the club chaplain Linda, who has been a critical part of the team offering an ear when players needed it the most.

But just putting players on the ice doesn't make a game happen, it takes an incredible team of volunteers, that I honestly believe we have the best team of volunteers of any ice hockey club I have been a part of. Thank you to each and every one of our volunteers that dedicate their weekends to allow us to put our games on each week.

It's the small things that usually go unnoticed, but everything from goal judges, game clocks, team sheets, to 50/50 sellers, match night announcers and DJ's all need to be there for every game, and we have had the best. So thank you once again to you all.

We couldn't put any of this together without the help of our sponsors, who allow us to be able to put a team on the ice. We cannot thank them all enough for their support. Thank you to YKK, The Coach Company, Cross Check Clothing, BASN. Planet Ice, Straight In, Sprakes & Sons, MPG Maintenance, University of Salford and the Halton Haven Hospice for everything they have done for us this season. Hopefully the first of many seasons together.

Thank you to the BASN team for the amazing Drop The Puck coverage each week.

And finally, the biggest thank you of all. You, the fans. The Wild Ones! You are the reason why we do it. The reason why we turn up every week. And the support and love we have received from you all this year cannot be put into words just how appreciated it has been.

When we needed that extra pickup and push, when we needed that backing you were always there.

Saying thank you for your support doesn't seem enough, but we hear every chant, every shout from the crowd and it is pushes every player to keep going.

Every team will tell their fans they have the best in the league, but the amazing travelling support we have at every game is something to behold, and the noise at every home game is always mentioned by other teams' coaches and fans.

We truly have the best fans in the league!

It has been an absolute honour to be a part of this team this season, and we have already started work on next season to make sure that this is just the start of good things to come. The Widnes Wild has always had a fine winning tradition, and I have no intention of letting that stop now.

Onwards and upwards, and big things are coming for the Wild.

Evan Coles receives the Player of the Month award for November
(Photo by Rebecca Clayton)

PLAYER OF THE MONTH AWARD

The highly popular Wild Player of the Month award was re-introduced this season and was voted on by the fans via an online Twitter poll at the end each calendar month of the season.

The full list of winners for the 2021/22 season were:

September: Vlads Vulcanovs
October: Liam Charnock
November: Evan Coles
December: Harrison Walker
January: Tom Stubley
February: Liam Charnock
March: Matty Barlow

Matty Barlow (#89) receives the Player of the Month award for March
(Photo by Geoff White)

24th April 2022: Barlow & Gilbert in England Call Up

Widnes Wild players Matty Barlow and Mikey Gilbert have been called up to join the England Under 23 team for a series of games to be played against Denmark this week.

The games will be played at Planet Ice Widnes this Thursday 28th April – face off 7pm – and at iceSheffield on Friday, 7.30pm start. Barlow will be playing in both matches while Gilbert will be acting as a coach on the bench for the game at Widnes.

The Under 23 team is part of the new "Recruit-Train-Retain" strategy that had been brought in to help the continued development of players aged 18 to 23 after they have passed out of the junior system.

The new team was launched at a training camp in Sheffield over the Easter weekend by England National Team Programme head Andy

Daintith and new Under 23 Head Coach Paul Glossop. Over 50 players were in attendance for a full day on Monday, with classroom sessions, video with GB coach Pete Russell and multiple on-ice sessions ending with a full scrimmage.

Matty Barlow is in his second spell with the Wild club, having joined earlier in the season. He has made a significant contribution to the team's achievements, helping them to a 3rd place finish in the Moralee Division and winning the Moralee Cup – and has scored 11 goals and 10 assists in 28 games.

Commenting on his selection for the England Under 23 team, Barlow said:

"Being asked to trial to potentially play for your country is an honour in itself and then to be told you are playing both games against Denmark is an experience I won't forget!"

"When I arrived at the camp on Monday, I was still upset about the Billingham games over the weekend and knowing that, after the season we've had – finishing 3rd and lifting a trophy – we should have finished our season in Leeds."

"The day camp alone was tough with 2 on ice sessions, a fitness test and a game to finish off. The competition on and off the ice from the boys was good to be a part of as it's pushing you through each drill and shift."

To hear that I've been selected for both games and one being on HOME ice in Widnes is one I'm looking too! I'll hopefully see many faces that I usually see week in week out too."

Mike Gilbert is another important member of the Wild Moralee Division team but he is also a key member of the coaching staff and is Head Coach of the Wild Junior Academy.

Gilbert will be one of the coaches on the bench for the England Under 23 game at Widnes on Thursday and he explained how it all came about:

"Andy Daintith and Paul Glossop asked me if I was interested in helping out on the coaching side with the England U23s team and I was extremely happy to be asked and, of course, I accepted. I wasn't expecting the call and it is a great thing to be asked to be a part of."

"What Andy and Paul have set up here is a really good development stepping stone for the young elite players in England which will only help further all of the players progression in their playing careers. It is a chance for the players to showcase their talent in a skilled team with the best of their country and age group, allowing for a further pathway to be made towards the national team."

"Paul, Andy and Matt Bradbury are all experienced and good coaches so the team is in great hands and it is an honour to be asked by them to work with them with the team that has been built."

"Denmark are a really well drilled and skilled ice hockey nation so the task at hand is a tough one but the work ethic and ability to play of the selected players is really good so it should be an exciting two games to say the least! To have one of the games at Widnes too is a bonus."

"Good luck to all the players and let's prove that England is progressing in the sport!"

Admission to both England Under 23 games is free and spectators are encouraged to go along and support this exciting new initiative.

The England U23 team that played against Denmark at Widnes
(Photo by Geoff White)

28th April: England U23 1 – Denmark U23 11 (at Widnes)
29th April: England U23 0 – Denmark U23 15 (at Sheffield)

The Planet Ice rink in Widnes hosted a prestigious international challenge match between the new England Under 23 team and Denmark U23s last Thursday – resulting in a 1-11 win for the visitors.

As well as hosting the event, further Widnes interest was provided by Wild NIHL player Matty Barlow having been selected for the England team and Academy Head Coach Mikey Gilbert who was helping on the bench.

Denmark took the lead in the 2nd minute and were 0-4 up by the time Solihull Barons player Jordan Jolly scored the only goal of the game for England on 14 minutes. A further goal from the visitors towards the end of the period saw them leading 1-5 at the first break.

Just 2 goals followed in the second period – both for Denmark – and four more unanswered strikes in the third period – including two in the last 60 seconds of the game – rounded off an impressive 1-11 win for the overseas visitors.

A second game between the two teams, played in Sheffield the following night saw a similar pattern with the marauding Danes coming out 0-15 winners.

Talking afterwards about his involvement in the two England matches, Matty Barlow said:

"The whole experience will be something I'll be proud of and remember for a lifetime. Opportunities like that don't come round so often and I was honoured to be selected to represent my country but also to wear the A on my jersey was special to me."

"The games against Denmark were really tough. It's whole different side of hockey I've never seen before – especially being out there on the ice with them. Their skating, puck movement and their general IQ of the game was something else."

"That was a whole new level of hockey and I think, personally, myself and the lads were blown away when we saw them play. As difficult as the games were, we showed heart and spirit throughout both games and showed why we were chosen to play for England."

"It has opened my eyes a lot more knowing the hard work Denmark put in to the game as players and it makes me want to push myself that extra step that I've not taken before."

"Thank you to the Widnes fans on Thursday night who made it extra special for me and the lads."

Mikey Gilbert and Matty Barlow in England uniform at the U23 game against Denmark at Planet Ice Widnes

(Photos by Geoff White)

Widnes GM Wez Spurrett presents Ken Armstrong and Tom Jackson with special awards for having passed 250 games for the Wild. (Photo by Mark Ferriss)

13th May 2022: Presentation Evening

The YKK sponsored Widnes Wild held their end of season presentation evening at the Village Club in Widnes on Friday evening.

It was the first time in three years that the fans, players, team staff and volunteers had been able to get together post season as the 2020 and 2021 events were not possible due to the Coronavirus pandemic and subsequent lockdown restrictions.

There had been, however, a set of virtual "Dippy" awards given out via Zoom back in 2020 when Shaun Dippnall decided to organise an unofficial ceremony for the players in a private video chat group.

Luckily there were no such hindrances this time around and the evening was able to take place in the traditional manner with music, buffet and lots of jollity and applause.

The Player Awards for the season went to:
- Defenceman of the Season – Thomas Stubley
- Forward of the Season – Vlads Vulkanovs
- Fans' Player of the Season – Harrison Walker

- Players' Player of the Season – Harrison Walker
- Coach's Most Improved Player – Tom Brierley
- Coach's Player of the Season - Liam Charnock

Supporters were also able to collect their "own and loan" shirts that had been sponsored for the duration of the season and have photos taken with their favourite players.

Wild netminder Harrison Walker (right – pictured here with Chris Wilcox) receives awards for both the Fans' Player of the Season and Players' Player of the Season

Coach's Most Improved Player Tom Brierley presents his "own & loan" home shirt to match volunteer Jennifer Hunt.

(Photos by Mark Ferriss)

Widnes Wild Ladies Team Photo – Season 2021/22.
Back Row: Beckie Elliott, Shannon Holt, Olivia Wilson, Jennifer Hickey, Leen de Decker, Natalie Buckles, Preston Gennoe, Karyn Cooper, Catherine Bowen Fell, Katie Adshead, Daisy Winstanley, Vanessa Crickmore Clarke. Front Row: Laura Marcroft, Danielle Skilander, Elizabeth Loss, Katie Fairclough, Emma Downe, Stephanie Drinkwater, Jemma Brown, Suzie Miller, Ellie-Bindi Walsh-O'Neill, Phoebe Patient, Ellen Tyrer. (Photo by Geoff White).

Widnes Wild Ladies Team

The Wild Ladies team had an eventful 2021/22 season in the Women's Premier League, gaining many friends, if not many points.

At the end of the 16-match campaign, they finished bottom of the league table with just 1 draw from 16 starts but that solitary statistic doesn't really tell the full story.

One thing to bear in mind is that they actually finished this season with THREE more points than they had managed the last time they played at this level.

Yes – they finished the 2018/19 season on minus 2 points after declining to play an away game against Chelmsford that had originally been scheduled to take place at mid-day in Chelmsford and then got moved to a Sunday night in East London at very short notice.

As seems to happen on a very regular basis, the team saw a sizable turnover of players during the summer with the arrival of a number of promising young talents to join the returning core squad.

However, a certain amount of experience was lost from the team as the top goal scorers from each of the past 2 seasons, Emma Pearson and Sav Sumner, along with Charlotte McPhee and Kat Garner all left for pastures new. Preston Gennoe came in from Coventry to counter this and Olivia Wilson – formerly of Whitley Bay – also contributed some experience at league level.

Giving the season fair reflection as a whole, the Wild Ladies should probably have won both their games against Nottingham, having led both home and away - and they possibly should have got results in the home games against Slough and the Firebees, when they put in a few good spurts late on but had left themselves too much to do in the latter stages.

For the rest, they came up against teams packed with current Elite League players – or, at least, players with Elite League experience - so it was never really much of a level playing field.

A few unwanted records left their mark on a generally "character-building" season – like losing 41-0 on aggregate over two games to runaway champions Bristol Huskies and going 206 minutes and 48 seconds without scoring a goal in a spell that saw 3 consecutive shut-outs

But on the whole, it was an enjoyable and uplifting experience for all those who were involved with the Wild Ladies team and, with all the promising young players who are now coming through from the impressive Wild Junior Academy – and who all gained much-needed game time this season - it will be fascinating to see how they might go onto to develop as a unit in the next few years.

WOMEN'S PREMIER LEAGUE
Season 2021/22

Final Table	GP	W	D	L	F	A	+/-	PIM	Pts
Bristol Huskies	16	15	1	0	150	7	143	123	31
Sheffield Shadows	16	11	1	4	106	39	67	54	23
Kingston Diamonds	16	10	2	4	75	27	48	136	22
Queen Bees	16	8	2	6	67	44	23	115	18
MK Falcons	16	9	0	7	83	56	27	130	18
Chelmsford Cobras	16	7	1	8	90	110	-20	161	15
Slough Sirens	16	4	0	12	54	124	-70	118	8
Nottingham Vipers	16	3	2	11	41	119	-78	145	8
Widnes Ladies	16	0	1	15	31	171	-140	78	1

Leading Points Scorers

Player	Team	GP	G	A	Pts	PIM
Ila Hobbins	Bristol Huskies	13	21	19	40	6
Eleanor Cooper	Sheffield Shadows	13	22	17	39	2
Jennifer Bolton	Chelmsford Cobras	16	25	12	37	4
Katie Edginton	Bristol Huskies	14	21	10	31	37
Rebecca Osman	Bristol Huskies	16	13	18	31	10
Jodie Attrill	Slough Sirens	15	19	10	29	6
Charmaine Easton	Chelmsford Cobras	15	18	11	29	41
Amiee O'Brien	MK Falcons	16	24	5	29	28
Hazel Taylor	Sheffield Shadows	13	11	18	29	0
Ellie Wallace	Bristol Huskies	11	14	15	29	4

Leading Netminders

Netminder	Team	GP	SA	GA	Sv%	SO
Mali Easton	Bristol Huskies	8	54	0	100.00%	6
Liberty Bird	Kingston / Sheff	10	269	5	98.14%	9
Gemma Davies	Bristol Huskies	11	140	5	96.43%	6
Sophia Voslinsky	Firebees	12	301	27	91.03%	1
Dawn Dickinson	Kingston Diamonds	13	116	11	90.52%	1

Widnes Ladies Team - Fixtures & Results

Date	Game	Home	H	A	Away	WDL
11/07/2021	Chall	Sheff Shadows	10	2	Widnes Ladies	L
24/07/2021	Chall	Widnes Ladies	7	9	Caledonia S Queens	L
28/08/2021	Chall	Widnes Ladies	1	11	Bracknell Firebees	L
10/10/2021	WPL	Chelmsfd Cobras	7	2	Widnes Ladies	L
30/10/2021	WPL	Slough Sirens	10	4	Widnes Ladies	L
06/11/21	WPL	Sheff Shadows	14	0	Widnes Ladies	L
14/11/2021	WPL	Nottm Vipers	5	5	Widnes Ladies	D
21/11/2021	WPL	Widnes Ladies	2	3	Nottingham Vipers	L
02/01/2022	WPL	Widnes Ladies	0	9	Kingston Diamonds	L
09/01/2022	WPL	Widnes Ladies	0	9	Sheffield Shadows	L
23/01/2022	WPL	Bristol Huskies	21	0	Widnes Ladies	L
06/02/2022	WPL	Widnes Ladies	4	13	Chelmsford Cobras	L
13/03/2022	WPL	Kingston Dias	15	0	Widnes Ladies	L
20/03/2022	WPL	Widnes Ladies	3	7	Firebees	L
03/04/2022	WPL	Widnes Ladies	4	7	Slough Sirens	L
01/05/2022	WPL	Widnes Ladies	0	20	Bristol Huskies	L
08/05/2022	WPL	Widnes Ladies	2	14	MK Falcons	L
15/05/2022	WPL	MK Falcons	9	3	Widnes Ladies	L
22/05/2022	WPL	Firebees	8	2	Widnes Ladies	L

Unofficial "Netminder Saves" Table – WPL 2021/22

Player	Team	SA	GA	Saves
Stephanie Drinkwater	Widnes Ladies	903	124	779
Gerry Park	Slough Sirens	642	78	564
Caitlin Woolley	Nottingham Vipers	586	86	500
Cherry Hambelton	Chelmsford Cobras	479	95	384
Kayliegh Doyle	MK Falcons	428	53	375
Kirsty Robson	Sheffield Shadows	368	39	329

Preston Gennoe (#53) topped the standings for goals, assists, points and PIM for the Wild Ladies team this season (Photo by Brian Noble)

Above left: Stephanie Drinkwater (#1) faced more shots in the WPL than any other netminder this season but also made more saves than anybody else -779. That's 215 more than Slough's Gerry Park who came second in the "saves made" table.

Above right: Player, coach and captain Leen de Decker was second highest points scorer for the season and her usual inspirational self both on and off the ice. (Photos by Geoff White)

Widnes Wild Ladies Team Player Statistics – Season 2021/22

Player	Women's Premier League					Challenge		Totals				
	GP	G	A	Pts	PIM	GP	Pts	GP	G	A	Pts	PIM
Preston Gennoe	12	7	4	11	26	1	1	13	8	4	12	26
Leen De Decker	14	6	3	9	4	1	0	15	6	3	9	4
Katie Fairclough	13	5	2	7	4	0	0	13	5	2	7	4
Catherine Fell	12	4	1	5	20	1	0	13	4	1	5	20
Jemma Brown	13	2	2	4	4	2	1	15	2	3	5	4
Charlotte Cramp	15	2	1	3	0	1	2	16	3	1	5	0
Kaitlyn Kerr	0	0	0	0	0	2	4	2	2	2	4	2
Karyn Cooper	14	0	2	2	0	1	0	15	0	2	2	2
Ellen Tyrer	14	1	1	2	2	1	0	15	1	1	2	2
Ellie Walsh-O'Neill	14	2	0	2	2	0	0	14	2	0	2	2
Jennifer Hickey	14	1	0	1	2	1	1	15	1	1	2	2
Danielle Skilander	8	0	1	1	2	1	1	9	1	1	2	2
Kathryn Garner	0	0	0	0	0	1	2	1	2	0	2	0
Katie Adshead	13	0	1	1	2	2	0	15	0	1	1	2
Natalie Buckles	9	0	1	1	4	2	0	11	0	1	1	4
Beckie Elliott	7	1	0	1	0	0	0	7	1	0	1	0
Suzanne Miller	14	0	1	1	0	2	0	16	0	1	1	0
Phoebe Patient	14	0	1	1	2	1	0	15	0	1	1	2
Olivia Wilson	11	0	1	1	0	1	0	12	0	1	1	0
Daisy Winstanley	7	0	1	1	0	0	0	7	0	1	1	0
Laura Marcroft	14	0	0	0	0	2	1	16	0	1	1	0
Sav Sumner	0	0	0	0	0	1	1	1	1	0	1	0
Sarah Aspinall	1	0	0	0	0	1	0	2	0	0	0	0
Vanessa C-Clarke	9	0	0	0	0	0	0	9	0	0	0	0
Emma Downe	7	0	0	0	0	2	0	9	0	0	0	0
Steph Drinkwater	14	0	0	0	0	0	0	14	0	0	0	0
Pamela England	1	0	0	0	0	1	0	2	0	0	0	0
Pauline Hayward	2	0	0	0	0	0	0	2	0	0	0	0
Shannon Holt	12	0	0	0	0	1	0	13	0	0	0	0
Charlotte Jackson	8	0	0	0	0	2	0	10	0	0	0	0
Elizabeth Loss	10	0	0	0	0	1	0	11	0	0	0	0
Charlotte McPhee	0	0	0	0	0	1	0	1	0	0	0	0

Netminder Statistics

		GP	SA	GA	SA%	SO
Stephanie Drinkwater	WPL	14	903	124	86.27%	0
Charlotte Jackson	WPL	8	220	47	78.64%	0
	Chall	2	98	20	79.6	0
	Totals	10	318	67	78.9	0

Note – the player statistics for the challenge game away to Sheffield Shadows on 11th July have never been made available.

The two challenge matches referred to here are 24th July v Caledonia Steel Queens and the informal training session on 28th August v Firebees. Neither of these games feature in the official EIHA statistics, so this is the only place that they are recorded.

Wild women's Kat Garner (#88) receives the MVP award from match timekeeper Rebecca Clayton (Photo by Paul Breeze)

Saturday 24th July 2021 – Challenge Match
Widnes Wild Women's Team 7- Caledonia Steel Queens 9

The Widnes Wild women's team were involved in a highly enjoyable sixteen goal thriller in their pre-season challenge game against the Edinburgh-based Caledonia Steel Queens at Planet Ice Widnes on Saturday, narrowly losing out 7-9.

This was the first home game for the Wild women since 1st March 2020 due to the various rink closures and Covid lockdowns and was the first time that fans had been able to see the team in action since they won the Division 1 North league title away in Dumfries, before the 2019/20 season was curtailed.

The Wild women's team iced a largely inexperienced development team against the Steel Queens - with several players who are new to competitive ice hockey and, indeed, 4 were making their home Wild debuts.

The match started well for Widnes with new player Kaitlyn Kerr opening the scoring with her first ever Wild goal after just three minutes. The Steel Queens equalised on 13 minutes but Widnes edged back again just 90 seconds later with a second goal for Kerr.

The lead only lasted 13 seconds, however as the Scots equalised again and the score remained 2-2 at the first period break.

Widnes scored with a superb strike from Sav Sumner on 23 minutes to restore the lead but, once again, they were pegged back by a goal from the visitors some 4 minutes later. The same thing happened again at the mid-point of the game when Charlotte Cramp scored her first goal for Widnes on 32 minutes and the Steel Queens came back to level on 38 minutes.

Just when it looked as if the game would remain a stalemate heading into the second period break, the Wild women scored again with a goal from Kat Garner with just 70 seconds left on the clock. She repeated the feat just 12 seconds into the 3rd period to put Widnes 6-4 up and show daylight between the two teams for the first time in the game.

There were hopes that the numerically superior Widnes team might start to pull away at this point but the Caledonia team had other ideas and they pulled one goal back within 90 seconds.

The game was completely turned on it head in the 46th minute when a mix up in defence allowed the Steel Queens to equalise and then they skated straight down the ice from the resulting face off to score again and take the lead. As if that wasn't bad enough, they did the same thing with their very next attack as well to score a third goal within 24 seconds of each other. This put them 6-8 in the lead and left the Wild women a lot to do in the latter stages of the game.

Widnes did pull a goal back through a Danielle Skilander strike on 53 minutes but any hopes of a late Wild fightback were dashed by another Steel Queens goal 3 minutes later.

Overall this was a very entertaining game – played in the very best of spirits and with only 2 PIM being handed out in total. The teams were for the most part pretty evenly matched and, save for the dramatic events of the 46th minute, the result could easily have gone either way.

The Edith Smith Memorial MVP awards were presented by match volunteer Rebecca Clayton and went to Mikanshi Ashok for the Steel Queens and Kat Garner for Widnes.

The Wild women's team that played against the Caledonia Steel Queens.

Back Row: Phil Pearson, Charlotte Cramp, Jemma Brown, Suzanne Miller, Kaitlyn Kerr, Natalie Buckles, Emma Downe. Front Row: Jennifer Hickey, Pamela England, Laura Marcroft , Danielle Skilander, Elizabeth Loss, Charlotte McPhee, Sav Sumner, Katie Adshead. Reclining: Charlotte Jackson (Photo by Paul Breeze)

11th July 2021: Sheffield Shadows 10 – Widnes Wild Women 2

This challenge game saw a development-based Widnes team take on the Sheffield Shadows WPL team at iceSheffield.

No game sheet was made available but we are reliably informed that Katie Fairclough and Natalie Buckles scored the Wild goals.

28th August: Wild Women – Bracknell Firebees

This was supposed to be a challenge game but, due to administrative difficulties at EIHA level, it was reclassified as a training session with players from Widnes and Bracknell all taking part as one big happy group.

Had goals been being counted, Bracknell would have won 1-11, with Preston Gennoe scoring for Widnes on her first appearance.

After the session, timekeeper Rebecca Clayton presented "Spirit Of The Training Session" awards to Alissa Mailes from Bracknell and Preston Gennoe from Widnes.

(Photos by Paul Breeze)

**Sunday 10th October 2021 – Women's Premier League
Chelmsford Cobras 7 – Widnes Wild Women's Team 2**

The Widnes Wild women's team put in a battling performance in their first game back in the Women's Premier League before ultimately losing out 7-2 to very a strong and experienced Chelmsford Cobras team away in Essex on Sunday.

The women's team has seen a lot of changes since they won the Division 1 (North) in their last league match all the way back in March 2020 and this game saw senior league debuts for Ellen Tyrer and Phoebe Patient - who had both previously played for the Wild Academy Under 15 mixed team, Jennifer Hickey and Charlotte Cramp.

Also new to the Wild women for this season were Preston Gennoe – formerly with Coventry Phoenix, Olivia Wilson who previously played with Whitley Bay and Beckie Elliott, who is back at Widnes after two seasons away.

Chelmsford were the first to score in this early face off game (12.15 start), taking the lead after just two minutes but Widnes were back on level terms just 4 minutes later with a goal from Beckie Elliott.

The Cobras edged ahead again on 9 minutes and the Wild women countered with an equaliser from Preston Gennoe on 15 minutes to leave the score standing at 2-2 at the first period break.

The Wild women were heavily outshot throughout this game but it took until 13 minutes into the second period for their stubborn defences to be breached again - when three quick-fire goals within 50 seconds of each other put the hosts well and truly in the driving seat.

At 5-2 after two periods, it looked as if the game was slipping away for the Wild women and they went further behind to a 6th goal on 44 minutes. The scoring was rounded off with a 7th goal for the Cobras with just 1 second left on the clock.

Netminder Stephanie Drinkwater performed wonders in the Wild goal to keep the score down in the latter stages, stopping an incredible 56 of the 63 shots that she faced. By way of the vaguaries of statistics, she ended up with a better "Save Percentage" for the game - with 88.89% - than the Chelmsford netminder, who had ended up on the winning side but who only had a 75% Save Percentage.

Saturday 30th October 2021 – Women's Premier League
Slough Sirens 10 – Widnes Wild Women's Team 4

The Widnes Wild women's team slumped to a 10-4 defeat away to Slough Sirens in the Women's Premier League on Saturday.

With a new look team from the side that won the Division 1 North title last season, the Wild women travelled to Berkshire with several experienced players missing but gave league debuts to Daisy Winstanley and Natalie Buckles.

Slough took the lead in the 8th minute but Widnes equalised on 13 with a goal from Katy Fairclough.

Two more goals for the Sirens – including one with just 40 seconds to go in the period - saw them leading 3-1 at the first break.

Slough scored twice more to give themselves a 5-1 lead before Fairclough once again found the net for Widnes but two more home goals late in the period already looked to have pretty much settled the game in Slough's favour.

However, a goal just two minutes from the restart from Charlotte Cramp – her first ever league goal – gave the Wild women some hope and she repeated the feat in the 55th minute to narrow the score to 7-4.

Three late goals from Slough gave the score an undeservedly one-sided feel but the Wild women gave a good account of themselves overall and will be pleased with an improved "shots on goal" tally of 37 for the match.

The Wild women have two more away games – at Sheffield this Saturday 6th November and Nottingham on 14th November – before they play their first home of the new campaign on Sunday 21st November when they take on the Nottingham Vipers at Planet Ice Widnes – 4.15pm face off.

Saturday 6th November 2021: Women's Premier League
Sheffield Shadows 14 - Widnes Wild Women's Team 0

The Widnes Wild women's team's steep learning curve in life back in the WPL continued on Saturday with a 14-0 defeat away to Sheffield Shadows.

This is a greatly changed team from the Wild women side that won the Division 1 North title back in the 2019/20 season and the combination of losing the highest goal scorers from the two previous seasons during the summer and the fact that they are now playing in a higher division always suggested that this season might be a bit of a challenge.

Continuing their policy of encouraging new talent, the Wild gave a league debut to Ellie Walsh–O'Neill, who had previously played with the Academy Under 18 mixed team.

Sheffield opened the scoring in the 6th minute and led 2-0 at the first period break. 4 unanswered goals followed in the second period and 8 in the third, which made the final result look a little more one-sided than the game actually was. Despite the high scoring tally, Charlotte Jackson put in a good performance in the Widnes net and stopped 48 of the 62 shots that she faced.

Sunday 14th November 2021 – Women's Premier League
Nottingham Vipers 5 – Widnes Wild Women's Team 5

The Widnes Ladies team picked up their first WPL point of the season with an exciting and highly entertaining 5-5 draw away to Nottingham Vipers on Sunday.

This was the best performance of the season so far with the Wild women outshooting their opponents by 46 to 33 and clearly demonstrates that the new look team - with a lot of new players since last season - is beginning to gel on the ice.

Nottingham took the lead after just 60 seconds of the game but Widnes equalised with a goal from Jennifer Hickey – her first for the club – on 7 minutes.

The Wild took the lead just 90 seconds later through Preston Gennoe and the score remained at 1-2 at the first period break.

This was a very closely contested game throughout with both teams having their chances but it was the Vipers who eventually made the next breakthrough with an equalising goal on 28 minutes.They then went on to retake the lead with a short handed goal 4 minutes later.

Parity was restored on 34 minutes when Catherine Bowen Fell fired in a third goal for Widnes and the game remained on a knife-edge at 3-3 after two periods.

The Wild women visibly upped their game in the last period and peppered the Nottingham goal with shots. They were rewarded in the 44th minute when Bowen Fell scored her second goal of the game to edge Widnes back into the lead.

The advantage was extended to 3-5 with a second goal from Gennoe with just 3 minutes left in the game, and it began to look as if the Wild women were going to secure their first win at WPL level since they beat the Vipers back in December 2017.

But there was drama late on as Nottingham pulled a goal back with just 90 seconds left to play – and then levelled the scores once more 24 seconds later.

The clock ticked down and the game finished as a 5-5 draw with both teams taking a point, which sees the Wild women move off the bottom of the WPL table.

The Widnes Ladies will be hoping to build on this result when they take on the Vipers again next Sunday 21st November in their first home game of the season at Planet Ice Widnes – 4.15 pm face off.

Leen de Decker (#88) scores for the Widnes Ladies against Nottingham
(Photo by Geoff White)

Sunday 21st November 2021: Women's Premier League
Widnes Ladies 2 – Nottingham Vipers 3

The Widnes Wild ladies team put in a battling performance in their first home game of the Women's Premier League season, narrowly losing out 2-3 to Nottingham Vipers at Planet Ice Widnes on Sunday.

After 4 away games in a row, this game had been keenly anticipated and there was a huge crowd in the rink to watch the resumption of rivalries between the same two teams that had drawn 5-5 in the Lace City last weekend.

This was a very good advert for women's ice hockey, with the two the teams very closely matched throughout. The game could have gone either way and the result remained in doubt until the very last second.

After a tense opening phase, Widnes took the lead after 6 minutes with a goal from Belgian international Leen de Decker and, despite mounting pressure from the Vipers' attack, the score remained 1-0 at the first period break.

The game was littered with niggly penalties for both sides and this seemed to affect the Widnes most as they found themselves having to defend shorthanded for sustained periods of play.

Nottingham scored their first goal of the game on a powerplay after just 46 seconds of the second period and then edged into the lead with a second strike 4 minutes later.

Widnes fought back and narrowly outshot the Vipers during the second period. Their mounting pressure was eventually rewarded when Jemma Brown fired in a goal on a delayed penalty call for slashing with just 26 seconds left in the second period – leaving the game on a knife edge with everything still to play for.

The third period continued in the similar end-to-end vein and Widnes were caught out at the back while pushing forward on a powerplay to concede a short handed goal in the 47th minute.

Both teams had numerous chances in the latter stages but impressive performances by the netminders at either end saw the rest of the game play out goal-less.

This result sees the Vipers move up into second place in the WPL table while Widnes remain 8th at this early stage of the season.

The Widnes Ladies are without a game now until the New Year when they take on Kingston Diamonds from Hull on 2nd January at Planet Ice Widnes – 4.15pm face off.

WW1 HEROINE REMEMBERED IN WILD LADIES' MOST VALUABLE PLAYER (MVP) AWARDS

The Widnes Ladies team will be honouring First World War inspirational woman Winifred Mabel Letts this season, following Wild club Poet In Residence Lucy London's decision to sponsor the Most Valuable Player awards this season in her memory.

It is the third year in a row that Lucy has sponsored the MVP awards for the Wild women's home matches and, in keeping with her other main activity – that of researching and raising awareness of the roles of women in the Great War – Lucy has once again decided to dedicate this year's awards to the memory of another such woman.

For the 2018/19 season, the Wild women MVP awards were dedicated to the memory of Sarah MacNaughtan who single-handedly set up and operated soup kitchens in the war zones on the western front, and in 2019/20, the awards were in honour of Merseyside born Edith Smith who became the country's first female warranted police officer during WW1 and later worked as a nursing assistant at a hospital in Runcorn.

Winifred Mabel Letts was born in Salford and she went to be a successful writer. During the First World War, she joined the Volunteer Aid Detachment and worked as a nurse at Manchester Base Hospital. She then trained as a medical masseuse – that is a physiotherapist in modern parlance – with the Almeric Paget Military Massage Corps. Winifred worked at Army camps in Manchester and Alnwick, Northumberland.

Talking about her choice of Letts to commemorate for this season's awards, Lucy said;

"As the Wild club have a connection with the Physio Department at Salford University for this season, I felt it appropriate to commemorate Winifred as she was born in Salford and became a medical masseuse – which was the forerunner of physiotherapy."

The first Winifred Mabel Letts memorial MVP awards of the season were presented at the home game against Nottingham Vipers on Sunday. The presentation was made by Widnes off ice game official Paul Breeze and the awards went to Sarah Kimber for the Vipers and Preston Gennoe for Widnes.

Paul Breeze presents the first Winifred Mabel Letts memorial MVP award of the season to Sarah Kimber of Nottingham Vipers

(Photo by Geoff White)

Wild's Preston Gennoe (#53) receives the MVP award from match timekeeper Rebecca Clayton (Photo by Paul Breeze)

Sunday 2nd January 2022 – Women's Premier League
Widnes Wild Ladies 0 – Kingston Diamonds 9

The Widnes Wild ladies team got the new year off to a low key start with a 0-9 defeat at the hands of the Kingston Diamonds at Planet Ice Widnes on Sunday.

The visitors opened the scoring straight from the face off with just 12 seconds gone on the clock and, having got that early boost, there was no stopping them.

They doubled the advantage on 6 minutes and were 0-3 up on 8 minutes – and a further goal late in the period saw Kingston leading 0-4 at the first break.

The Wild women visibly upped their game in the second period and enjoyed much more puck possession and shots on goal. However, they weren't able to make the most of their chances and were continually thwarted by a solid Diamonds defence and their netminder, who was in fine form.

Three straight goals in the second period for Kingston's Elizabeth Saunders put the game well beyond the reach of the Widnes side and, from then on, it was more of a case of damage limitation.

In the Widnes net, Stephanie Drinkwater pulled off some superb saves to keep the score down and was only beaten once more - in the 56th minute. The game finished 0-9 to Kingston but that scoreline makes it sound a little more one-sided than it actually was.

Looking at the positives, this is a new-look team playing in a higher division and the mix of youth and experience will continue to gel as the players get more games together under their belts. The match saw home WPL debuts for Charlotte Cramp and Daisy Winstanley and further promising performances from the young trio of Ellen Tyrer, Phoebe Patient and Ellie Walsh O'Neill - who are also all in their first season of senior competitive hockey.

The Winifred Mary Letts MVP awards – which have been sponsored this season by Wild Poet In Residence Lucy London in memory of the First World War poet and medic – went to Megan Day for Kingston and Preston Gennoe for Widnes and were presented by match volunteer Rebecca Clayton.

The Widnes Ladies are at home again this Sunday 9th January when they take on league leaders Sheffield Shadows at Planet Ice Widnes – face off 4.15pm.

Wild's Phoebe Patient (#44) receives the MVP award from match volunteer Lynda Bird
(Photo by Paul Breeze)

Sunday 9th January 2022 – Women's Premier League
Widnes Wild Ladies 0 – Sheffield Shadows 9

The Widnes Wild ladies team put in a spirited performance but slumped to a 0-9 defeat at the hands of league leaders Sheffield Shadows at Planet Ice Widnes on Sunday.

The visitors opened the scoring with just 47 seconds gone on the clock and, having got that early boost, there was no stopping them. They doubled the advantage on 2 minutes and were 0-3 up on 5 minutes – and further goals late in the period saw Sheffield leading 0-5 at the first break.

The Wild women steadied the ship somewhat in the second period and put some good attacks together themselves but were unable to make the most of their chances. They managed to keep the Sheffield offence at bay for a good 13 minutes before the next goal went in on 33 minutes and this was followed up by another strike 90 seconds later and another 2 minutes after that.

Sheffield led 0-8 after two periods but, with their bench short on numbers, they began to lose steam in the final period – although their healthy lead by that time allowed them to ease off a bit.

The third period yielded just one goal – scored by Sheffield on 57 minutes and the game finished 0-9 to the visitors.

The Winifred Mabel Letts MVP awards – which have been sponsored this season by Wild Poet In Residence Lucy London in memory of the First World War poet and medic – went to Eleanor Cooper for Sheffield and Phoebe Patient for Widnes and were presented by match volunteer Lynda Bird.

The Widnes Ladies are next in action on Sunday 23rd January when they travel to take on the Bristol Huskies at the new Planet Ice rink in Bristol – face off 5.30pm – and are next at home on Sunday 6th February, then they entertain the Chelmsford Cobras at Planet Ice Widnes – face off 4.15pm.

Shannon Holt (#7) and Natalie Buckles (#9) in action against the Huskies away in Bristol (Photo by Flyfifer Photography)

Sunday 23rd January – Women's Premier League
Bristol Huskies 21 – Widnes Ladies 0

The Widnes Wild Ladies team continued their steep learning curve in the Women's Premier League with a 21-0 drubbing away to Bristol Huskies on Sunday.

The Huskies are favourites to take the league title this season and have a 100% record with, now, 5 wins from their 5 games overall, having conceded just 2 goals in total.

The Wild women lost their two top goalscorers from the previous two seasons during the summer and have put together a completely new look squad for their return to this higher division - so this first ever trip to the new Bristol rink, taking on the relocated Swindon Topcats team containing several players with Elite League experience, was always likely to be a bit of a test.

Bristol took the lead after just 90 seconds of the game and were 10-0 up by the end of the first period. After two periods it was 17-0 and four more goals went in during the third.

In the Widnes goal, plucky Stephanie Drinkwater – who was just getting over an illness - faced an incredible 101 shots and impressively managed to save 80 of them.

The Wild Ladies are next in action on Sunday 6th February when they take on Chelmsford Cobras at Planet Ice Widnes, 4.15pm face off.

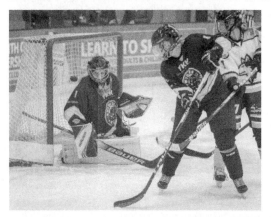

Overworked Wild netminder Stephanie Drinkwater (#1) in action away at the new Planet Ice rink in Bristol against the Huskies.

(Photo by Flyfifer Photography)

The Widnes Ladies team away at Bristol. Back row: Laura Marcroft, Katie Adshead, Catherine Fell, Olivia Wilson, Pauline Hayward, Charlotte Cramp, Natalie Buckles, Karyn Cooper, Katie Fairclough, Emma Downe, Ellie Walsh-O'Neill, Shannon Holt

Front row: Jennifer Hickey, Suzie Miller, Leen de Decker, Elizabeth Loss, Daisy Winstanley, Phoebe Patient, Ellen Tyrer. Front: Jemma Brown, Stephanie Drinkwater (Photo by Flyfifer Photography)

Wild's Elizabeth Loss (#34) receives the MVP award from match mascot Lilly Miller (Photo by Paul Breeze)

Sunday 6th February 2022 – Women's Premier League
Widnes Ladies 4 – Chelmsford Cobras 13

The Widnes Wild Ladies team put in a much improved performance against the Chelmsford Cobras at Planet Ice Widnes on Sunday but unfortunately lost out 4-13 in a highly entertaining game at Planet Ice Widnes on Sunday.

The visitors took the lead after just 32 seconds but the roof of the rink was metaphorically raised at 6.22 when Katie Fairclough fired in an equaliser for the Wild, thus ending an extended goal drought for the Widnes team.

Having failed to score at all in their last 3 games – albeit against the leading teams in the division and very strong opposition – you have to go back to 21st November and 39 minutes 34 seconds into the home game against Nottingham when the Wild women last found the back of the net – this was quite a momentous event for the players and their fans.

Indeed it represented an incredible 206 minutes 48 seconds of playing time without a goal – quite possibly some sort of unwanted Women's Premier League record - so you can easily appreciate why this Fairclough strike was so enthusiastically received.

Chelmsford hit back almost immediately, however, restoring the lead just 30 seconds later and went on to build up an impressive 1-5 advantage by the end of the first period.

A 6th goal for the Cobras 2 minutes from the restart edged them further ahead but Widnes heads did not drop and they went on to have their best spell of the game.

A goal for Ellen Tyrer – her first ever in senior competitive hockey – on 24 minutes received as big an ovation as Fairclough's earlier marker and then Catherine Fell fired in just 50 seconds later to draw the Wild ladies back to 3-6.

There then followed a highly frenetic 9 minute phase with both teams having plenty of chances on goal and Widnes looking ever likely to further narrow the deficit.

The next goal, however - when it came - fell to Chelmsford and they quickly scored two more follow up strikes. Preston Gennoe fired in for Widnes on 35 minutes leaving the score at 4-9 to the visitors at the second period break.

4 unanswered goals for Chelmsford in the third period made the overall scoreline appear more one-side than the game actually was and the Wild women can draw a lot of positives from this performance.

The Winifred Mabel Letts memorial MVP awards sponsored by Poet In Residence Lucy London went to Tegan Hyatt for Chelmsford and Elizabeth Loss for Widnes and were presented by match mascot Lilly Miller.

The Widnes Wild Ladies team are next in action on Sunday 13th March when they travel to face Kingston Diamonds in Hull – 12.30 (noon) face off, They are next at home on Sunday 20th March when they entertain the Queen Bees at Planet Ice Widnes, 4.15pm face off.

Sunday 13th March 2022 – Women's Premier League
Kingston Diamonds 15 - Widnes Ladies 0

The Widnes Wild Ladies team had a difficult trip to Humberside in the Women's Premier League on Sunday, suffering a 15-0 drubbing at the hands of the Kingston Diamonds.

Kingston opened the scoring after just 45 seconds and were leading 6-0 by the first period break. 6 more unanswered goals followed in the second period and 3 more in third.

In fairness to the Wild women, all but one of the Kingston goals were scored by players who also play regularly for the Diamonds Elite League team, so this was hardly an even-sided encounter.

Many of the Widnes players are in their first ever season of competitive hockey and very few others have much experience at WPL level. One positive note from the game was that netminder Charlotte Jackson managed to turn away an incredible 68 of the 83 shots that she faced during the 60 minutes.

The Wild Ladies team are at home on Sunday 20th March when they take on the Firebees at Planet Ice Widnes, 4.15 pm face off.

Charlotte Cramp (#29) and Preston Gennoe (#53) celebrate the latter's first goal against the Firebees (Photo by Geoff White)

Sunday 20th March 2022 – Women's Premier League
Widnes Wild Ladies 3 – Firebees 7

The Widnes Wild Ladies team put in an impressive performance against the Slough-based Firebees at Planet Ice Widnes on Sunday and were ultimately unlucky to finish up on the wrong end of a 3 –7 scoreline.

After a close opening phase, the visitors opened the scoring in the 5th minute and raced to a 0-3 lead before Catherine Fell pulled a goal back for the Wild women with just 44 seconds left in the first period.

The second period was a much closer run affair with the Firebees being restricted to one single goal on 26 minutes, which was cancelled out by a superb strike by Preston Gennoe to leave the score standing at 2-4 at the second period break.

A second goal for Gennoe early in the third period narrowed the deficit to just one goal and Widnes really were flying.

As they pushed forward looking for an equaliser, however, they were caught out at the back and the Firebees struck again to make the score 3-5.

This was really a most entertaining game to watch and, although the visitors had the upper hand for long spells, the Wild Ladies never gave up and, on another day, might well have snatched a result.

As it was, two late goals gave the scoreline a more uneven feel than the game deserved but the Wild women have plenty of positives to look back on.

In the Widnes goal, Stephanie Drinkwater faced an incredible 93 shots but managed to turn away 86 of them for an impressive 92.7 save percentage.

The Winifred Mabel Letts memorial MVP awards sponsored by Poet In Residence Lucy London went to Phebe Dodd for the Firebees and Laura Marcroft for Widnes and were presented by off-ice match official Paul Breeze.

The Widnes Wild Ladies team are next in action on Sunday 3rd April when they entertain the Slough Sirens at Planet Ice Widnes, 4.15pm face off.

Laura Marcroft (#93) picked up the MVP award for the home game against the Firebees (Photo by Geoff White)

Jemma Brown (#66) receives the MVP award from match volunteer Tricia Holt (Photo by Paul Breeze)

Sunday 3rd April 2022 – Women's Premier League
Widnes Wild Ladies 4 – Slough Sirens 7

The Widnes Wild Ladies team staged an heroic late comeback in their Women's Premier League home game against the Slough Sirens at Planet Ice Widnes on Sunday but, unfortunately, it wasn't quite enough to prevent them ultimately slipping to a 4-7 defeat.

This was a very entertaining game from start to finish and, apart from an unfortunately subdued middle period, was closely contested throughout.

Slough took the lead after 5 minutes but were otherwise kept at bay by some stubborn defending and a superb display of netminding by the Wild's Stephanie Drinkwater, who turned away 25 shots in the first period to keep the score at 0-1 at the first break.

The visitors scored again just 49 seconds into the second period and with the Wild women constantly pressing forward to try and break their duck but having no luck in front of goal, went on to add 4 more unanswered goals.

With the scoring standing at 0-6 after two periods, a rout looked on the cards but, 4 minutes into the third period, Ellie Walsh O'Neill fired in her first ever competitive goal for Widnes and the atmosphere around the rink noticeably lifted.

Slough scored again on 48 minutes to extend the lead to 1-7 but the Wild players had a definite spring in their step and looked a lot more dangerous going forward.

A goal from Jemma Brown on 52 minutes boosted the mood and further strikes - from Kate Fairclough and Leen De Decker on 55 and 58 minutes respectively – sparked further hopes of a dramatic late comeback but, unfortunately, the clock ticked down far too quickly.

Had the game gone on for an extra 5 minutes or so, the result might have been different - but the Wild Ladies can be especially proud of their performance in the latter stages as they out-shot their opponents by 22 to 15 and won the final period 4-1.

The Winifred Mabel Letts memorial MVP awards sponsored by Poet In Residence Lucy London went to Aniko Gaal - who previously played for the Budapest Stars in the European Women's Hockey League back in her native Hungary – and Jemma Brown for Widnes, and were presented by match volunteer Tricia Holt.

The Widnes Wild Ladies team are next at home on Sunday 1st May when they take on runaway league leaders Bristol Huskies in the Women's Premier League at Planet Ice Widnes – 4.15pm face off.

Charlotte Cramp (#29) receives the MVP award from match timekeeper Thomas Horner (Photo by Paul Breeze)

Sunday 1st May 2022 – Women's Premier League
Widnes Wild Ladies 0 – Bristol Huskies 20

The Widnes Wild Ladies team put in a plucky performance against the table topping Bristol Huskies in their Women's Premier League game on Sunday at Planet Ice Widnes but ultimately slumped to a 0-20 defeat.

The new Huskies team have taken the league by storm this season, are undefeated in all 14 games they have played to date and only conceded 7 goals in the process so Sunday's game was always going to be a bit of an uphill struggle for the Wild women.

As it turned out, Widnes started the game very well and gave as good as they got in the opening minutes. It took the recently crowned league champions until the 9th minute to breach the Wild defences and two further goals saw them leading at the first period break.

Despite the one sided scoreline, this was a very entertaining game to watch and the Wild players never let their heads drop once and kept battling right through to the final buzzer.

8 unanswered goals followed for the visitors in the second period and 9 more in the third but the Widnes netminding duo of Stephanie Drinkwater and Charlotte Jackson put in an heroic performance, stopping an incredible 79 shots out of the eye-watering 99 that they faced over the course of the game.

The Winifred Mabel Letts memorial MVP awards sponsored by Poet In Residence Lucy London went to Nora Egri for Bristol and Charlotte Cramp for Widnes, and were presented by match volunteer Thomas Horner.

The Widnes Wild Ladies team play their last home game of the season this Sunday 8th May when they take on Milton Keynes Falcons in the Women's Premier League at Planet Ice Widnes – 4.15pm face off.

Preston Gennoe (#53) joins in the celebrations for Leen de Deckers (#5) goal against Milton Keynes (Photo by Brian Noble)

Sunday 8th May – Women's Premier League
Widnes Wild Ladies 2 – Milton Keynes Falcons 14

The Widnes Wild Ladies team put in a stirring performance in their last Women's Premier League home game of the season but it ultimately wasn't enough to prevent them slumping to a 2-14 defeat at the hands of the Milton Keynes Falcons at Planet Ice Widnes on Sunday.

It has been a difficult season for the Wild women, having been promoted to the higher division after previously winning the Division 1 North title and their new look – and largely youthful - team has regularly found themselves up against long established WPL teams, with some squads packed with players with Elite League experience.

The game on Sunday started well for Widnes and they matched the visitors blow for blow in the early stages.

Milton Keynes scored the first goal in the 5th minute but Widnes looked to have equalised shortly afterwards but were not quite able to force the puck over the goal line.

Had that goal gone in, things might have been a lot different but, instead, the Falcons struck back and two quick fire goals just 30 seconds apart around the 7 minute mark to give them a commanding early lead.

The Wild women kept plugging away but their efforts to push forward left them exposed at the back and they were susceptible to breakaways and long shots. Three more unanswered goals for the Falcons saw them leading 0-6 at the end of the first period, leaving Widnes with a lot of catching up to do.

The home side had a much better second period, keeping the number of shots down on embattled netminder Stephanie Drinkwater while putting more pressure on the Falcons' defence and goal. Two more Milton Keynes goals followed but then Widnes had their brief period of domination.

A superb strike from season top scorer Preston Gennoe gave the Wild women their opening goal of the game on 34 minutes and captain Leen de Decker made it 2 for Widnes just 30 seconds later.

This got the crowd on their feet and, despite the score standing at 2-8, there were still hopes of a Widnes comeback at this point as the Milton Keynes team had a very short bench and were quite likely to tire in the latter stages.

The home team pushed forward again in the hope of further reducing the deficit but, despite creating numerous chances in front of goal, were unable to make any of them count and it remained a 2-2 period.

A superhuman effort by the numerically challenged Falcons saw them edge further ahead in the third period with a 9th goal on 44 minutes and then a 10th 5 minutes after that. Widnes heads did not drop at any point and the team continued to battle until the final buzzer.

4 more unanswered goals in the final 10 minutes gave the final score a slightly more one-sided look than the game deserved but the Wild Ladies can still be pleased with what they have achieved this season.

Rhianna Holt presents the MVP award to Vanessa Crickmore-Clarke
(Photo by Paul Breeze)

The Winifred Mabel Letts memorial MVP awards sponsored by Poet In Residence Lucy London went to Samantha Ruff for Milton Keynes and Vanessa Crickmore-Clarke for Widnes, and were presented by match volunteer Rhianna Holt.

The Wild Ladies have two more away games still to play to round off their WPL season. They are away to Milton Keynes this Sunday 15th May – 6.30 pm face off - and then travel to Slough to face the Firebees in Slough the Sunday after.

Ellie Walsh-O'Neill (#3) opened the scoring for the Wild Ladies away at Milton Keynes (Photo by Brian Noble)

Sunday 15th May – Women's Premier League
Milton Keynes Falcons 9 – Widnes Wild Ladies 3

The Widnes Wild Ladies team continued their challenging Women's Premier League season with a 9-3 defeat away to Milton Keynes Falcons on Sunday.

Having lost 2-14 to the same opposition at home the previous weekend, this could definitely be viewed as an improvement - and that is testified by the increase in shots on goal that the Widnes team managed to create as well as the reduction in shots conceded over the course of the game.

The Wild actually scored first with a goal from Ellie Walsh-O'Neill in the 7th minute but that strike was cancelled out by an MK equaliser just 52 seconds later.

The Falcons edged ahead 3 minutes after that but a goal from Widnes captain Leen de Decker levelled the scores again on 12 minutes.

All was looking good until the hosts re-took the lead on 17 minutes and then a hammer blow just 11 seconds from the buzzer saw them take a 4-2 advantage into the first period break.

The second period saw Milton Keynes pile on the pressure and they were rewarded with 3 unanswered goals to lead 7-2 at the second break.

Widnes pulled a goal back through de Decker on 50 minutes but that was as good as it got for the battling Wild women as two late goals for the hosts rounded off the scoring and topped off a 9-3 victory.

Wild netminder Stephanie Drinkwater once again performed miracles in the Widnes goal to keep the score down and managed to save 50 of the 59 shots that she faced.

The Widnes Ladies play their last game of the season away to the Firebees in Slough next Sunday 22nd May – face off 6pm.

That game will have added significance for the Firebees as victory will confirm their place in the end of season playoffs.

The Wild Ladies team for their last game of the season away to the Firebees in Slough: Back row: Jennifer Hickey, Olivia Wilson, Charlotte Cramp, Leen de Decker, Karyn Cooper, Ellie Walsh-O'Neill
Front row: Katie Adshead, Laura Marcroft, Ellen Tyrer, Katie Fairclough, Suzie Miller, Preston Gennoe, Shannon Holt. Front: Stephanie Drinkwater

Sunday 22nd May: Firebees 8 – Widnes Wild Ladies 2

The Widnes Wild Ladies team finished off their roller-coaster Women's Premier League season with an 8-2 defeat away to the Firebees in Slough on Sunday.

The home side took the lead 3 minutes into the game but Widnes drew level just 2 ½ minutes later with a superb goal from Katie Fairclough. Two more quick-fire goals followed for the Firebees just 40 seconds apart and then a further strike late in the period saw them leading 4-1 at the first break.

Widnes had a much better second period in terms of puck possession and shots on goal but found themselves caught out at the back as they pushed forward trying to narrow the deficit. This led to three answered goals, which gave the Firebees a commanding 7-1 lead at the mid-way point of the game.

Wild heads did not drop, however, and the continued Widnes pressure was eventually rewarded with a goal from team captain Leen de Decker on 38 minutes.

There was just one goal in the 3rd period – for the home side in the 44th minute to bring the score to 8-2 – and embattled netminder Stephanie Drinkwater put in another heroic performance in the Widnes goal to keep the score down.

In fact, she turned away an incredible 60 of the 68 shots that she faced over the course of the game and actually finished the match with a better overall "save percentage" than her opposite number on the winning team.

Another interesting statistic saw the Wild women not incur any penalties for the third game in a row – quite possibly some sort of record - and this was, indeed, the 7th out of 16 league games overall this season where they managed to go penalty free.

Sunday's win over Widnes meant that the Firebees made sure of a 4th place finish in the league table and thus clinched the final spot in the end of season play offs.

Guildford Lightning – Women's Elite League Play Off Champions
(Photo by Flyfifer Photography)

Women's Play Off Weekend At Widnes – 4th/5th June

Widnes staged another top level ice hockey event at the weekend with the Women's Trophy Weekend being played at the Planet Ice rink.

An incredible 10 games played over the two days saw many of the country's top women players meet in the semi finals of the Women's Elite League (WEL), Women's Premier League (WPL) and English Division 1 (D1) on Saturday, with 4 finals on Sunday.

In the Women's Elite League semi finals, runaway league champions Solihull Vixen surprisingly lost 4-6 to Guildford Lightning - the only time they have lost to them in 5 meetings this season - while 4th place finishers Streatham Storm beat league runners up Queen Bees 2-1. This meant, unusually, that neither of the WEL's top teams of recent seasons would appear in the play off final this year.

In the Women's Premier League semi finals, league champions Bristol Huskies – who had gone through the regular season unbeaten in all 16 games - beat Kingston Diamonds 3-0 and Sheffield Shadows beat the Firebees 4-1.

In the North v South Division 1 semi-finals, D1 North champions Whitley lost 3-5 to D1 South runners up Streatham and Solway Sharks Ladies lost 2-8 to S1 champions Swindon Topcats to set up an all-south final.

Sunday saw 4 back-to-back finals. In the Elite League decider, Guildford Lightning won their first ever WEL title with a 5-2 victory over Streatham Storm, while the WPL final saw Bristol Huskies make it a league and play-off double with a 7-3 win over Sheffield Shadows.

In the all-south Division 1 final, the Swindon Topcats beat Streatham 7-0 to secure the play off crown to go with their league title. They also win promotion to the Women's Premier League for next season, depending on any league restructuring.

The Under 16 girls national play off saw southern champions Haringey-based London Capitals beat north winners Kingston Diamonds 2-1.

EIHA Director Faye Andrews presents the Women's Premier League Play Off trophy to members of the double winning Bristol Huskies team

(Photo by Flyfifer Photography)

WILD WOMENS TEAM END OF SEASON AWARDS

Following the conclusion of the women's ice hockey season, the Wild Ladies team held their end of season awards night.

The award for most points for the season went to Preston Gennoe, who joined the club last summer. She finished the campaign with 8 goals and 4 assists from 13 league and challenge games and also topped the club standings in penalties with 26.

The Wild Ladies player, coach and captain Leen de Decker – who holds the all time goals and appearances record in the World Championships for her native Belgium – was named Best Forward of the Year while the Best Defence award went to Vanessa Crickmore-Clarke.

Overworked netminder Stephanie Drinkwater – who faced more shots in the WPL than any other netminder this season, but also made more saves than anybody else – was Players' Player of the Season and Charlotte Cramp was Coach's Player of the Season.

Ellie Walsh-O'Neill - playing her first season of senior competition - was named most improved player.

The Wild Ladies team are now taking a well –earned break and will resume training for the new season on 19th July. New players – especially anybody with league experience – are always welcome.

Widnes Wild Academy Under 18 – Season 2012/22
(Photo by Geoff White)

WILD ACADEMY UNDER 18 SEASON REVIEW

The Wild Academy Under 18 team can look back on a successful season having finished in a highly creditable 3rd place in the 5–team Under 18 North 2 league table.

This is the first time that the Under 18 team has completed a full season of competition after their debut 2019/20 campaign was cut short by the Covid pandemic and to have held their own among longer established teams with much more experience is a great credit to the players and coaches.

The Wild youngsters finished the season with a 50/50 playing record, having won 8 and lost 8 of their 16 league games. By far the best team in the league were Sutton U18, who finished top of the table with 30 points while runners up Sheffield notched 23 points.

The Wild were unable to beat Sutton in any of their 4 league meetings but they did beat Sheffield 9-2 in their final encounter – and also achieved a clean sweep over Solihull and 3 wins from 4 games with Nottingham. This gave them 16 points overall and they finished well clear of Nottingham who got 9 and Solihull who finished bottom with 2.

Luke Mullarkey was the Wild's leading points scorer for the season with 14 goals and 21 assists from 13 games and he finished 4th in the overall league scoring standings.

George Plevin was the top Widnes sniper with 23 goals (plus 7 assists) for a 7th place overall finish while Jake Meehan, Ben McLellan, Adam Case, Joel Bark, Ellis Mahar and Liam Yarwood also made it into double figures.

Calam Barber and Ellie Green shared the netminding duties over the course of the season and finished up with Save Percentages of 85.06 and 80.88 respectively.

Left:
George Plevin
scored 23 goals in
11 games (Photo
by Geoff White)

Left to right: Cody Ogden, Ben McLellan, Jake Meehan, Joel Bark, Luke Mullarkey all played in the North Showcase teams (photo by Widnes Wild Academy)

Final League Table Under 18N2 – Season 2021/22

	GP	W	D	L	F	A	+/-	PIM	Pts
Sutton 18	16	15	0	1	179	44	135	233	30
Sheffield	16	11	1	4	131	63	68	237	23
Widnes Wild	16	8	0	8	101	113	-12	404	16
Nottingham 18	16	4	1	11	58	125	-67	281	9
Solihull U18	16	1	0	15	33	157	-124	191	2

Leading Points Scorers

Player	Team	GP	G	A	Pts	PIM
Jacob Frost	Sutton 18	16	41	24	65	14
Nathan Mead	Sutton 18	16	26	35	61	2
Jack Straw	Sutton 18	16	28	17	45	6
Luke Mullarkey	Widnes Wild	13	14	21	35	16
Edward Harley	Sutton 18	14	11	21	32	29
Lewis Kimpton	Sutton 18	13	17	13	30	6
George Plevin	Widnes Wild	11	23	7	30	43
Jacob Brammer	Sheffield	9	16	10	26	30
William Gibbons	Sutton 18	14	6	19	25	2
Owen Jenkinson	Sutton 18	15	16	9	25	14
Regan Kidd	Sheffield	12	7	17	24	0
Jake Meehan	Widnes Wild	15	9	14	23	0

Leading Netminder

Netminder	Team	GP	SA	GA	Sv%	SO
Ryan Mansfield	Nottingham	13	456	51	88.82%	0
Jack Mickevicius	Sutton 18	16	185	21	88.65%	6
Deacon Hardy	Sheffield	13	262	36	86.26%	2
Calam Barber	Widnes Wild	8	348	52	85.06%	0
Joshua Halkyard	Sutton 18	16	142	23	83.80%	3
Owen Crowder	Nottingham	14	449	74	83.52%	0
Scarlett Richardson	Sheffield	9	181	30	83.43%	0
Ellie Green	Widnes Wild	9	319	61	80.88%	0
Chi Yln Lam	Solihull U18	13	636	130	79.56%	0

Wild Academy Under 18 Team
Fixtures & Results – Season 2021/22

Date	Game	Home			Away	WDL
03/10/2021	U18N2	Sutton	14	4	Widnes Wild	L
09/10/2021	U18N2	Solihull	4	9	Widnes Wild	W
16/10/2021	U18N2	Widnes	14	2	Solihull	W
23/10/2021	U18N2	Widnes	2	12	Sheffield	L
30/10/2021	U18N2	Nottingham	5	6	Widnes Wild	W
06/11/2021	U18N2	Widnes	8	3	Nottingham	W
07/11/2021	U18N2	Sheffield	11	3	Widnes Wild	L
13/11/2021	U18N2	Solihull	1	6	Widnes Wild	W
11/12/2021	U18N2	Widnes	7	15	Sutton	L
08/01/2022	CH	Widnes	10	1	Leeds	W
22/01/2022	U18N2	Widnes	10	4	Solihull	W
29/01/2022	U18N2	Widnes	9	4	Nottingham	W
30/01/2022	U18N2	Sheffield	8	3	Widnes Wild	L
06/02/2022	U18N2	Sutton	4	1	Widnes Wild	L
12/03/2022	U18N2	Widnes	4	16	Sutton	L
19/03/2022	U18N2	Widnes	9	2	Sheffield	W
09/04/2022	U18N2	Nottingham	8	6	Widnes Wild	L

Wild Academy Under 18 Team Player Statistics
Season 2021/22

	Under 18 League					Challenge		Totals				
	GP	G	A	Pts	PIM	GP	Pts	GP	G	A	Pts	PIM
Luke Mullarkey	13	14	21	35	16	1	4	14	16	23	39	16
George Plevin	11	23	7	30	43	1	0	12	23	7	30	43
Jake Meehan	15	9	14	23	0	1	4	16	10	17	27	0
Ben Mc Lellan	8	6	10	16	81	1	3	9	8	11	19	81
Rory Sillery	11	10	6	16	4	1	1	12	11	6	17	4
Adam Case	10	9	5	14	66	1	4	11	12	6	18	66
Joel Bark	15	5	8	13	14	1	1	16	5	9	14	14
Ellis Mahar	15	7	3	10	68	1	0	16	7	3	10	68
Liam Yarwood	14	7	3	10	6	0	0	14	7	3	10	6
Cody Ogden	10	6	3	9	6	1	0	11	6	3	9	6
Reid Ryan	14	2	6	8	4	1	0	15	2	6	8	4
Liam Eaton	8	0	6	6	0	1	0	9	0	6	6	0
Michael Price	12	3	3	6	27	1	0	13	3	3	6	52
Bram Coghlan	16	0	5	5	2	1	0	17	0	5	5	2
William Calcutt	12	0	3	3	24	1	0	13	0	3	3	26
Alain Barthelemy	15	0	2	2	0	1	0	16	0	2	2	0
Charlie Evans	10	0	1	1	29	1	0	11	0	1	1	31
Robert Georgescu	9	0	1	1	2	1	1	10	1	1	2	2
Damien Regan	15	0	1	1	4	1	0	16	0	1	1	4
Ellie Green	9	0	0	0	2	1	0	10	0	0	0	2
Jaxon Kirk-Jones	1	0	0	0	0	0	0	1	0	0	0	0
Ricards Konons	5	0	0	0	0	1	0	6	0	0	0	0
Phoebe Patient	1	0	0	0	0	1	0	2	0	0	0	0
Calam Barber	8	0	0	0	0	1	0	9	0	0	0	0
Ellen Tyrer	1	0	0	0	0	1	0	2	0	0	0	0
Alex Faulkner	0	0	0	0	0	1	0	1	0	0	0	0

Netminders			GP	SA	GA	Sa%	SO
Ellie Green		League	9	319	61	80.88%	0
Calam Barber		League	8	348	52	85.06%	0
		Chall	1	12	1	91.67%	0
		Total	**9**	**360**	**53**	**85.30%**	**0**

Wild Academy Under 18 Team Match Reports

3rd October: Sutton U18s 14 – Wild Academy U18s 4

The Wild Academy Under 18 team lost 14-4 to Sutton U18s in their opening game of the season away at iceSheffield on Sunday.

Widnes actually took the lead after just 4 minutes with a goal from Luke Mullarkey but Sutton equalised 3 minutes later and went on to lead 5-1 at the first period break.

Widnes scored again right from the restart through Mullarkey again and he fired in his hat-trick goal on 34 minutes. Unfortunately 4 more goals in between meant that the hosts led 9-3 after two periods.

The third period saw a Widnes goal for George Plevin and 5 goals for Sutton, leading to a 14-4 final score.

9th October: Solihull U18s 4 – Wild Academy U18s 9

The Wild Academy Under 18 team picked up their first win of the new season with a 4-9 victory away to Solihull U18s on Saturday.

Two goals within the first 90 seconds from George Plevin gave the Wild an early lead but they were pegged back to 2-2 by the 5th minute. A 12th minute strike from Rory Sillery put Widnes back into the lead and the score remained 2-3 at the first period break.

Goals from Ben McLellan and Adam Case (2) edged the Wild further ahead in the second period but Solihull didn't give up and, by the next break, the score stood at 4-6 to Widnes.

The hosts visibly tired in the third period and the Wild were able to press home their numerical advantage on the bench to score three unanswered goals – from Plevin, Michael Price and Joel Bark to round off the victory.

Ellie Green performed well in the Widnes net, turning away 25 of the 29 shots that she faced.

16th October: Wild Academy U18s 14 – Solihull U18s 2

The Wild Academy Under 18 team picked up their second win in a row with a 14-2 victory over the Solihull U18s at Planet Ice Widnes on Saturday.

Adam Case opened the scoring for Widnes in the 3rd minute and Ben McLellan made it 2-0 on 11 minutes. Solihull pulled a goal back but unanswered strikes from Jake Meehan, Case again, and Ellis Mahar put the Wild youngsters well and truly in the driving seat and the score stood at 5-1 at the first period break.

A goal from Wild captain Luke Mullarkey just 25 seconds from the restart put them 6-1 up and George Plevin made it 7-1 before Solihull were able to pull a goal back for themselves.

In the second half of the game, it was all Widnes and a goal from Mullarkey and two more from Plevin in the second period, followed by more from Mahar, Case (2), Plevin and Meehan in the third handed the Wild a comprehensive victory.

The Widnes top scorer for the game was George Plevin with 3+4, while Adam Case hit 4+1.

The win leaves the Wild in third place in the North Under 18 league table with a game in hand over the top two teams.

They are next in action this Saturday 23rd October when they face league leaders Sheffield at Planet Ice Widnes, 5pm face off.

23rd October: Wild Academy U18s 2 – Sheffield U18s 12

The Wild Academy Under 18 team lost 2-12 at home to league leaders Sheffield at Planet Ice Widnes on Saturday.

They actually put in a good performance and were not as out-played as the final score might suggest but Sheffield got the early breakthrough and were 0-3 up before Rory Sillery scored the first Widnes goal on 16 minutes.

By the time George Plevin scored the Wild's second goal on 32 minutes, Sheffield were leading 2-7 and the game looked pretty much over as a contest.

Another second period goal followed for Sheffield – plus 4 more in the third - and Widnes slumped to their first defeat in three games.

Despite the defeat, the Wild Under 18 team remain in third place in the league table behind Sheffield – who have a 100% record this season - and Sutton.

30th October: Nottingham U18s 5 – Wild Academy U18s 6

The Wild Academy Under 18 team consolidated their 3rd place position in the league table with a well-fought 5-6 win away over Nottingham U18s at the National Ice Centre on Saturday.

Nottingham scored first with just 47 seconds gone in the game and went on to outshoot the Wild by 24 to 6 in the first period. However Calam Barber put in an impressive display in the Widnes net and the score remained 1-0 at the first break.

Ben McLellan equalised for the Wild just 46 seconds into the second period and a goal from Cody Ogden – who was making his U18s debut and playing up a level from his normal age group – three minutes later put Widnes into the lead.

Two goals for Nottingham later in the period left the score standing at 3-2 to the hosts at the second period break with plenty still left to play for.

Nottingham edged further ahead with a goal on 44 minutes but Widnes fought back and two goals within 35 seconds of each other – from Liam Yarwood and Rory Sillery - put them back on level terms

The Wild took the lead again with a second goal of the night on 54 minutes from Sillery, only to see that cancelled out by another Nottingham strike two minutes later.

With three minutes left to play, and the teams locked together at 5-5, the tension around the rink was unbearable and then with just 32 seconds left on the clock, Liam Yarwood slotted in his second goal of the game to retake the lead for Widnes.

Nottingham removed their netminder in favour of an extra attacker for the remaining 30 seconds but it was to no avail and the Wild youngsters held out for the win.

Widnes U18s remain in third place in the league table with 6 points from their 5 games to date. They are next in action this Saturday 6th November when they take on Nottingham U18s at Planet Ice Widnes – 5pm face off.

6th November: Wild Academy U18s 8 – Nottingham U18s 3

7th November: Sheffield U18s 11 – Wild Academy U18s 3

The Wild Academy Under 18 team picked up their 4th win of the season with an 8-3 win over Nottingham Under 18s at Planet Ice Widnes on Saturday.

This was a very entertaining game – if a little on the physical side – and the Wild youngsters were clearly the better team for much of the game, outshooting the visitors by 71 to 25 over the 60 minutes.

Michael Price opened the scoring for Widnes after 5 minutes and goals from Cody Ogden – playing his second game of the day, having also iced in the Under 16s win over Manchester Storm beforehand - and Joel Bark saw them leading 3-0 at the first break.

A goal from team captain Luke Mullarkey just 33 seconds into the second period extended the Widnes lead to 4-0 but Nottingham eventually found the back of the net for themselves on 28 minutes.

A powerplay strike from Ogden at the midway point of the game restored the four goal lead but then two quick goals from the visitors just 70 seconds apart narrowed the score to 5-3 with 20 minutes left to play.

The third period was littered with penalties for both sides and a series of fights saw 3 Widnes players and 2 Nottingham players expelled from the game with match bans.

In between the various scuffles, Widnes scored 3 unanswered goals – from Ben McLellan, George Plevin and Mullarkey again to finish off the game.

On Sunday the Wild Under 18s lost 11-3 away to league leaders Sheffield. Liam Yarwood scored twice for Widnes, with the other goal coming from Luke Mullarkey.

The Academy U18s remain third in the league table after the weekend's matches.

13th November: Solihull Under 18s 1 – Wild Academy U18s 6

The Wild Academy Under 18 team moved into second place in the league table with a sensational 1-6 win away to Solihull U18s on Saturday.

Widnes opened the scoring with a 6th minute goal from team captain Luke Mullarkey and were 3-0 up by the first period break courtesy of strikes from Cody Ogden and Rory Sillery.

Solihull pulled a goal back right at the start of the second period but Widnes further extended the lead with goals from Jake Meehan and Liam Yarwood to lead 1-5 after 40 minutes' play.

A goal from Ellis Mahar on 45 minutes wrapped up the scoring for the game and the Widnes youngsters were able to celebrate their 3rd win in 4 matches.

With no other Under 18 games being played at the weekend, the result sees the Wild team move into second place in the table, just 2 points behind leaders Sheffield. They have 10 points from their 8 games to date but have played more matches then the other teams.

The Wild Under 18s are now without another game until 11th December so next weekend the spotlight falls on the Under 14 team who are at home to league leaders Leeds at Planet Ice Widnes on Saturday.

Widnes are second in the league table with 3 wins from their 4 games to date and are level on points with Leeds. The game faces off at 3.20 pm and admission is free.

11th December: Wild Academy U18s 7 – Sutton U18s 15

The Wild Academy Under 18 team lost ground on the teams at the top of the league table with a 7-15 home defeat to Sutton U18s at Planet Ice Widnes on Saturday.

Sutton took the lead after 90 seconds of the game but Ben McLellan equalised on 5 minutes and the Wild youngsters gave as good as they got in the earlier stages. However 4 unanswered goals in the first period and two more early in the second put the game beyond the reach of the Wild and by the time that Reid Ryan scored a short handed goal for Widnes, they were already 1-7 behind.

A burst of three goals within 90 seconds of each other – from George Plevin, Jake Meehan and Luke Mullarkey – gave the Wild some hope but Sutton countered again and the score was 5-11 after two periods.

The third period saw Widnes goals from Cody Ogden – playing his second game of the day having also played for the Under 16s immediately beforehand - and Adam Case but 4 more strikes for Sutton meant that the visitors were able to go back to Nottinghamshire with a comprehensive 7-15 victory.

8th January – Wild Academy U18s 10 – Leeds U18s 1

The Wild Academy Under 18 team got the new year off to a great start with a 10-1 challenge game win over the Leeds Under 18 team at Planet Ice Widnes on Saturday.

Leeds do not have a league team at Under 18 level yet so this was a good opportunity for their players in that age group to have a try-out together and it was a good work too for the Wild youngsters who otherwise would have 6 weeks without a game before their next league fixture later this month.

Widnes opened the scoring on 5 minutes with a goal from Luke Mullarkey and the same player doubled the lead just 60 seconds later. Further goals from Adam Case and Robert Georgescu meant that Widnes led 4-0 at the first period break.

Two more Widnes goals followed in the second period – from Case and Jake Meehan – and the Wild Academy looked well on top.

The third period had yet more goals with 4 for Widnes – from Ben McLellan (2), a hat-trick goal for Case and a fine strike by Rory Sillery – and a late consolation for Leeds which deprived Wild netminder Calam Barber of what would have been a well earned shut-out.

22nd January: Wild Academy U18s 10 – Solihull U18s 4

The Wild Academy Under 18 team beat the league's bottom team Solihull Under 18s 10-4 at Planet Ice Widnes on Saturday.

Solihull actually took an early lead and were 0-3 up by the first break but the Wild youngsters eventually found their mojo and 6 unanswered second period goals – from Ellis Mahar (2), Rory Sillery (2), Adam Case and Luke Mullarkey put them well in charge.

The goal rush continued in the third period with strikes from Reid Ryan, Cody Ogden – playing his second game of the afternoon - and Ben McLellan and then Sillery scored his hat-trick goal to round off the Wild tally in the 58th minute.

Solihull picked up a late goal with 51 seconds left on the clock and the game finished in a comprehensive 10-4 victory for Widnes.

Tempers boiled over in the third period and several fights broke out – including an unseemly melee at the final buzzer

The Wild Under 18s are next in action this Saturday 29th January when they are at home to Nottingham U18s at Planet Ice Widnes – 5pm face off.

29th January: Wild Academy U18s 9 - Nottingham U18s 4

30th January: Sheffield U18s 8 – Wild Academy U18s 3

The Wild Academy Under 18 team had a mixed weekend with a 9-4 home win over Nottingham Under 18s at Planet Ice Widnes on Saturday and then losing 8-3 away to Sheffield U18s on Sunday.

In the game on Saturday, Widnes opened the scoring on 2 minutes with a goal from Liam Yarwood. Nottingham hit back with two quick goals but with further goals from Michael Price and George Plevin it looked as if the Wild would be leading 3-2 at the first period break. However a last gasp goal for the visitors with just 1 second left on the clock left the game all tied up at 3-3.

Widnes had by far the better of the second period and 4 unanswered goals - from Joel Bark, Yarwood again, and two more from Plevin - gave them a commanding 7-4 lead after 40 minutes' play.

Two more goals followed for Widnes – a third in a row for Plevin to make it 4 in the game for him and then one from Jake Meeghan. Nottingham fired in a late short handed consolation with two minutes left to play but the match finished in a 9-4 win to Widnes.

In the away game on Sunday, Sheffield took the lead in the 2nd minute and were 4-0 up by the end of the first period. Widnes scored straight from the restart through George Plevin but three more Sheffield goals quickly followed.

A strike from Luke Mullarkey on 36 minute pulled the score back to 7-2 and Plevin added his second just a minute later but the hosts score again in the last minute of the period to round off the goal action for the game.

6th February: Sutton U18s 4 – Wild Academy U18s 1

The Wild Academy Under 18 team lost out 4-1 away to second place Sutton U18s on Sunday.

Sutton took the lead on 11 minutes and led 2-0 before Adam Case scored the only Widnes goal of the game on 18 minutes.

Two more goals for the home side in the second period rounded off the scoring for the game and the Academy U18s now have two weeks to regroup before they play the same opposition, also away, in Sheffield on 20th February.

12th March: Wild Academy U18s 4 – Sutton U18s 16

The Wild Academy Under 18 team lost 4-16 at home to Sutton U18s at Planet Ice Widnes on Saturday.

Widnes actually got off to a flying start with a goal from Jake Meehan after just 14 seconds but 4 straight goals for Sutton saw them leading 1-4 at the first period break.

Three more goals followed for the visitors giving them a 1-7 lead before George Plevin fired in for the Wild on 26 minutes. Things got a bit rough and a series of fights broke out which left Widnes short-handed for long spells. Sutton made the most of this by firing in 5 unanswered powerplay goals to lead 2-12 by the mid-point of the third period.

Two more goals followed for the Wild – from Ellis Mahar and Luke Mullarkey – but it did little to stem the flow and Sutton ended up 4-16 winners.

19th March: Wild Academy U18s 9 – Sheffield U18s 2

The Wild Academy Under 18 team put in a superb display to beat second placed Sheffield U18s 9-2 at Planet Ice Widnes on Saturday.

Jake Meehan put the Wild ahead after 4 minutes and scored a second goal less than 60 seconds later. Sheffield pulled a goal back but an 18th minute strike from George Plevin saw Widnes lead 3-1 at the first break.

Sheffield scored first in the second period to narrow the deficit but goals from Plevin again and Luke Mullarkey edged the Wild further ahead to lead 5-2 after two periods.

The third period was all Widnes and four straight goals from George Plevin – to give him an impressive 6 in the game – swept the Wild youngsters to a comprehensive 9-2 victory.

9th April: Nottingham U18s 8 - Wild Academy U18s 6

The Wild Academy Under 18 team rounded off their regular season schedule with an 8-6 defeat away to Nottingham Under 18s on Saturday.

Widnes had to travel to the Lace City with a weakened team and only had 10 skaters and 1 netminder on their bench - compared with 18 +2 for the home side - so this was always going to be a bit of a struggle, despite playing against a team that they had already beaten three times this season.

The game started close enough with Nottingham opening the scoring in the 6th minute and Widnes equalising through a Jake Meehan goal 90 seconds later. The host struck again and two goals late in the period saw them leading 3-1 at the first break.

Joe Bark pulled a goal back for the Wild on 25th minutes but this was countered by another strike for Nottingham and then a 5th goal on 35 minutes handed the hosts a clear lead.

A 6th goal for Nottingham just 40 seconds into the 3rd period looked to have the game all sewn up but two quick-fire markers for Widnes – from Ellis Mahar and Rory Sillery - just 15 seconds apart dragged them right back into contention with the score standing at 6-4.

Widnes out-shot Nottingham by 59 to 48 over the course of the game and peppered the home goal with an incredible 30 shots in the last period but were unable to make the most of their chances.

Two more Nottingham goals re-established the gap but the Wild youngsters managed to put in a late burst and score two more of their own – from Sillery and Bark – to keep the scoreline looking respectable.

The result makes no difference to the Wild's final position in the league table. They finish in a very creditable 3rd place out of 5 teams with 8 wins and 8 defeats from their 26 games, some way behind champions Sutton and runners up Sheffield.

Widnes Wild Academy Under 16 Team Photo – Season 2012/22
(Photo by Geoff White)

WILD ACADEMY UNDER 16 SEASON REVIEW

The Wild Academy Under 16 team had a superb season in the highly competitive 9-team Under 16 North Division 2, finish 3rd in the league table on league table and winning 12 of their 16 matches.

They finished just 2 points behind runners up Sheffield and only 5 points behind league champions Leeds, who went through the season unbeaten.

Apart from home and away defeats to Leeds, the only team to take a point off Widnes all season was Sheffield, meaning that the Wild youngsters notched up impressive home and away victories over local rivals Blackburn and Manchester Storm and long established teams such as Solihull, Nottingham and Sutton.

The leading points scorer for the season was Liam Yarwood with 30 goals and 8 assists in 18 league and challenge games while Cody Ogden was a close second with 23+11.

Netminder Harry Bird, played in all 18 matches as did Yarwood, Luke Alston and Samuel Hockey.

Jaxon Kirk Jones was the top Penalty taker with 31 minutes from 13 league and challenge games.

Above Left: Liam Yarwood (#25) played 18 games for the Academy Under 16s and 14 games for Academy Under 18s in the 2021/22 Season.(Photo by Geoff White)

Above Right: Under 16s ever-present netminder Harry Bird (Photo by Lynda Bird)

Above: Cody Ogden (#40) played 17 times for the Under 16s and 11 times for the Under 18s (Photo by Geoff White)

Final League Table Under 16N2 – Season 2021/22

	P	W	D	L	F	A	+/-	PIM	Pts
Leeds Jr Knights	16	15	1	0	122	27	95	44	30
Sheffield	16	13	1	2	113	23	90	173	27
Widnes Wild	16	12	1	3	113	43	70	129	25
Mcr Storm	16	9	1	6	108	68	40	100	19
Nottingham	16	7	1	8	84	63	21	201	15
Sutton	16	7	0	9	91	99	-8	79	14
Solihull	16	2	1	13	38	122	-84	114	3*
Grimsby	16	2	1	13	43	144	-101	60	2*
Blackburn	16	1	1	14	25	148	-123	189	1*

Top Points Scorers

Player	Team	GP	G	A	Pts	PIM
Thomas Milnes	Mcr Storm / BLA	15	40	10	50	42
Jay Musson	Leeds Junior Knights	14	28	11	39	10
Liam Yarwood	Widnes Wild	16	27	8	35	12
Jake Wigginton	Leeds Junior Knights	15	17	17	34	0
Daniel Ulik	Sutton	15	22	11	33	0
Edgars Vengis	Leeds Junior Knights	15	16	17	33	0
Cody Ogden	Widnes Wild	15	22	10	32	18
Owen Cutts	Sutton	16	23	8	31	10

Top Netminders

	Team	GP	SA	GA	Sv%	SO
Oliver Coote	Sheffield	10	185	9	95.14%	4
Callum Pike	Sheffield	12	73	6	91.78%	3
James Adamson	Leeds Knights	15	292	27	90.75%	3
Harry Bird	Widnes Wild	16	345	43	87.54%	1
Liam Lane	Mcr Storm	15	446	63	85.87%	3
Jack Hargreaves	Sutton / Not	15	617	101	83.63%	0

WILD ACADEMY UNDER 16 TEAM

Fixtures & Results – Season 2021/22

Date	Game	Home	Score	Score	Away	WDL
25/09/2021	U16N2	Widnes	13	1	Blackburn	W
02/10/2021	U16N2	Leeds	9	1	Widnes	L
16/10/2021	U16N2	Widnes	14	2	Solihull	W
06/11/2021	U16N2	Widnes	7	6	Mcr Storm	W
28/11/2021	U16N2	Grimsby	1	13	Widnes	W
11/12/2021	U16N2	Widnes	6	7	Leeds	L
15/01/2022	U16N2	Nottingham	1	2	Widnes	W
22/01/2022	U16N2	Widnes	5	2	Nottingham	W
13/02/2022	U16N2	Blackburn	0	8	Widnes	W
19/02/2022	U16N2	Widnes	4	4	Sheffield	D
27/02/2022	U16N2	Sheffield	2	1	Widnes	L
06/03/2022	U16N2	Solihull	1	9	Widnes	W
12/03/2022	U16N2	Widnes	11	2	Grimsby	W
02/04/2022	U16N2	Widnes	4	1	Sutton	W
09/04/2022	U16N2	Sutton	3	10	Widnes	W
23/04/2022	U16N2	Mcr Storm	1	5	Widnes	W
24/04/2022	CH	Widnes	5	5	Leeds	D
07/05/2022	CH	Leeds	6	1	Widnes	L

Wild Academy Under 16 Team Player Statistics
Season 2021/22

	Under 16 League N2					Challenge		Totals				
	GP	G	A	Pts	PIM	GP	Pts	GP	G	A	Pts	PIM
Liam Yarwood	16	27	8	35	12	2	3	18	30	8	38	14
Cody Ogden	15	22	10	32	18	2	2	17	23	11	34	18
Thom. Warburton	13	10	10	20	8	2	0	15	10	10	20	8
Jaxon Kirk-Jones	11	9	10	19	29	2	1	13	9	11	20	31
Jared Knowles	13	14	3	17	2	2	8	15	19	6	25	2
Luke Alston	16	8	8	16	4	2	2	18	9	9	18	4
Nathan Wilson	6	10	2	12	8	0	0	6	10	2	12	8
Aidan Lamb	11	2	6	8	2	2	9	13	7	10	17	2
Adam V/Yecsey	12	5	2	7	4	1	0	13	5	2	7	4
Samuel Hockey	16	0	6	6	2	2	0	18	0	6	6	2
Tristan Lewis	15	0	5	5	0	2	0	17	0	5	5	2
Theo Georgiou	2	3	1	4	2	0	0	2	3	1	4	2
Reece O'Brien	11	0	4	4	2	1	0	12	0	4	4	2
Porter Harrop	10	1	2	3	2	2	0	12	1	2	3	4
Harrison Lightfoot	12	3	0	3	2	1	0	13	3	0	3	2
Dylan Mcgee	11	0	3	3	20	1	0	12	0	3	3	22
Alfie Gilhooley	6	0	2	2	0	1	0	7	0	2	2	0
Harry Bird	16	0	1	1	0	2	0	18	0	1	1	0
Samuel Daintith	14	0	1	1	12	2	0	16	0	1	1	14
Nicholas Highcock	4	0	0	0	2	0	0	4	0	0	0	2
Declan Marston	4	0	0	0	0	0	0	4	0	0	0	0
Charles Shearn	2	0	0	0	0	0	0	2	0	0	0	0
Calam Barber	0	0	0	0	0	1	0	1	0	0	0	0

Netminder

		GPI	SA	GA	SA%	SO
Harry Bird	League	16	345	43	87.54%	1
	Chall	2	64	11	82.81%	0
	Total	**18**	**409**	**54**	**86.60%**	**1**
Calam Barber	Chall	1	12	1	91.67%	0

Wild Academy Under 16 Team Match Reports

25th September: Wild Academy U16s 13 – Blackburn U16s 1

The Wild Academy Under 16 team got their new season off to a flying start with an 18-1 hammering of near neighbours Blackburn at Planet Ice Widnes on Saturday.

However, due to the Junior League rules about one-sided contests, official scoring is suspended once one team or the other gets 12 goals ahead (8 goals at U12 level) - so this match will be recorded on the league table as a 13-1 win for Widnes.

Saturday 2nd October: Leeds U16s 9 – Wild Academy U16s 1

The Wild Academy Under 16 team lost 9-1 away to Leeds U16s on Saturday.

It wasn't a particularly one sided game as the "shots on goal" count was 33 to Leeds and 24 to Widnes but the home side were able to make more of their chances over the course of the match.

Widnes actually scored first – with a goal from Luke Alston in the 10th minute and the score remained 0-1 to the Wild at the first period break.

Leeds overturned the deficit straight from the restart with two goals within 10 seconds of each other and went on to lead 4-1 by the end of the second period.

The superior numbers on the home bench pressed home their advantage in the final period as the Wild players began to tire and 5 more unanswered goals produced a final score that wasn't necessarily a true reflection of the game overall.

16th October 2021: Wild Academy U16s 14 – Solihull U16s 2

The Wild Academy Under 16 team moved up to 4th place in the league table with a 14-2 win over Solihull Under 16s at Planet Ice Widnes on Saturday.

Liam Yarwood opened the scoring for Widnes after 2 minutes and further goals from Luke Alston and Cody Ogden made it 3-0 before

Solihull managed to find the back of the net themselves. A second goal for Ogden left the score at 4-1 at the first period break.

Second period from goals from Alston, Yarwood (2) and Nathan Wilson put the Wild youngsters well in control with an 8-1 advantage and then a further 6 goals in the third period from Yarwood (2), Ogden, Wilson (2) and Adam Vigh-Yecsey rounded off the scoring for Widnes. A late goal for Solihull gave them something more to cheer about but the game finished at 14-2 to the Wild.

The top scorers for Widnes were Liam Yarwood with 5+1 and Cody Ogden with 3+2. Luke Alston hit 2+2 while Nathan Wilson contributed a hat-trick 3+0.

6th November 2021: Wild Academy U16s 7 - Mcr Storm U16s 6

The Wild Academy Under 16 team made it 3 wins from 4 starts this season with a sensational 6-5 win over league leaders Manchester Storm U16s at Planet Ice Widnes on Saturday.

Cody Ogden opened the scoring in the 4th minute, Liam Yarwood added a second three minutes later and then Ogden fired in another on 11 minutes to give the Wild a 3-0 lead. The Storm pulled a goal back in the dying seconds of the first period and then scored again with just 25 seconds gone in the second to put themselves right back in the game.

A second goal from Yarwood edged Widnes further ahead again and then two goals within 12 seconds of each other on 25 minutes – from Nathan Wilson and Aidan Lamb put Widnes 6-2 up.

Manchester rallied after this and hit two goals in to leave the score at a tantalisingly close 6-4 with one period left to go.

A powerplay goal for the Storm just 45 seconds into the third period narrowed the score yet further to 6-5 and they equalised on 35 minutes, tying the score at 6-6 with 10 minutes left to play.

Widnes bounced straight back from this setback and the match was won by a superb goal from Nathan Wilson – his second of the game – straight from the face off and the Wild held off Manchester's last ditch attacks to secure a well earned victory.

The visitors actually outshot Widnes by 38 to 28 in this game and Wild netminder Harry Bird did well to keep out 32 shots out of the 38.

28th November: Grimsby U16s 1 – Wild Academy U16s 13

The Wild Academy Under 16 team moved up into second place in the league table after a comprehensive 1-13 win away over Grimsby on Sunday.

Widnes took the lead after just 27 seconds with a goal from team captain Thomas Warburton and further strikes from Luke Alston, Jared Knowles and Adam Vigh-Yecsey saw the Wild leading 0-4 at the first period break.

Grimbsy scored their only goal of the game in the 19th minute but a second period hat trick from Liam Yarwood plus more goals from Vigh-Yecsey and Knowles extended the Widnes lead to 1-9 after two periods.

Two more goals for Warburton and two for Knowles made this look like an easy victory for Widnes, but Grimsby put up a good fight and Wild netminder Harry Bird did well to keep out all but 1 of the 29 shots that he faced, finishing up with an impressive 96.55 save %.

The result sees the Wild Under 16s move ahead of Manchester Storm in the league table, level on points with leaders Leeds – who they play next at Planet Ice Widnes on 11th December.

11th December: Wild Academy U16s 6 – Leeds U16s 7

The Wild Academy Under 16 team lost their top of the table clash against Leeds U16s by the narrowest of margins, falling to a 6-7 defeat at Planet Ice Widnes on Saturday.

Leeds started the game the better side and were 0-3 up before Widnes scored their first goal through Cody Ogden on 10 minutes. A Liam Yarwood strike just 15 seconds before the buzzer narrowed the score to 2-3 at the first break but Leeds re-established the two goal cushion with a goal 3 minutes from the restart.

Two quick goals from Nathan Wilson briefly put Widnes level at 4-4 but another response saw the visitors take a narrow lead into the final period.

Two more goals early in the third put Leeds 4-7 ahead and two later markers from Liam Yarwood – to complete his hat-trick - were not enough to overturn the deficit.

15th January 2022 – Nottingham U16s 1 – Wild Academy U16s 2

The Wild Academy Under 16 team picked up a superb 1-2 win away to Nottingham Under 16s on Saturday.

Widnes opened the scoring on 12 minutes with a goal from Nathan Wilson and the score remained 0-1 at the first period break.

This was a very closely matched game and could have gone either way - and there were plenty of chances at both ends but the second period played out goal-less leaving the Wild youngsters with the narrowest of advantages heading into the final period.

Nottingham equalised on 34 minutes but Widnes hit back with a goal, from Jaxon Kirk-Jones – his debut strike for the club - just 70 seconds later and that turned out to be the winning goal.

Harry Bird put in an excellent display in the Widnes goal – almost getting a shut out - and saving 22 of the 23 shots that he faced.

22nd January: Wild Academy U16s 5 – Nottingham U16s 2

The Wild Academy Under 16 team beat Nottingham Under 16s 5-2 at Planet Ice Widnes on Saturday. Liam Yarwood opened the scoring for Widnes after just 25 seconds of the game and the score remained 1-0 at the first period break.

Nottingham equalised early in the second period but a second goal for Yarwood restored the advantage and then two more quick goals – within 62 seconds of each other - from Cody Ogden and Jaxon Kirk-Jones – handed Widnes a 4-1 lead.

Nottingham scored again early in the third period but a strike from Jared Knowles rounded off the scoring for the game and the Wild youngsters were able to celebrate a well-deserved 5-2 victory

The Wild Academy U14s are at home to Coventry U14s on Saturday 29th January at Planet Ice Widnes - 3.20pm face off – while the U12s are away at Leeds the same day - 4.20pm start.

13th February: Blackburn U16s 0 – Wild Academy U16s 8

The Wild Academy Under 16 team moved up to third in the league table after a 0-8 away win over Blackburn U16s on Sunday.

Team captain Thomas Warburton put Widnes ahead after just 80 seconds of the game and further goals from Jared Knowles, Luke Alston and Warburton again gave them a 0-4 lead at the first period break.

Jaxon Kirk-Jones edged the Wild further ahead early in the second period and further strikes from Warburton and Knowles (both notching up hat tricks) put the game well beyond the reach of the numerically inferior Blackburn side.

In the Wild net, Harry Bird put in an excellent performance to secure a 19-shot shut out.

19th February: Wild Academy U16s 4 – Sheffield U16s 4

The Wild Academy Under 16 team played out a thrilling 4-4 draw with league leaders Sheffield Under 16s at Planet Ice Widnes on Saturday.

The game was very closely fought throughout and with very little to choose between the two sides. The visitors eventually took the lead midway through the first period and the score remained 0-1 at the first break.

Liam Yarwood equalised for the Wild youngsters 4 minutes into the second period and the game remained finely balanced at the second break with 15 minutes left to play.

Sheffield edged back into the lead on 33 minutes and then extended the advantage 2 minutes after that but Cody Ogden narrowed the gap for Widnes on 37 minutes to leave the score standing at 2-3 with 8 minutes to go. A further exchange of goals – including a second strike from Ogden - saw the score at 3-4 with 5 minutes left to play and Jaxon Kirk-Jones salvaged a point for the Wild with a goal on 40 minutes to tie the score.

The result leaves the Wild youngsters in 3rd place in the league table, 4 points behind Sheffield but with a game in hand.

27th February 2022: Sheffield U16s 2 - Wild Academy U16s 1

The Wild Academy Under 16 team lost 2-1 away to Sheffield Under 16s on Sunday.

The hosts took the lead after just two minutes but Cody Ogden equalised for the Wild midway through the second period.

This was a very close game throughout, played between two very well matched teams. The decisive breakthrough came on 36 minutes when Sheffield scored what would turn out to be the winning goal.

6th March: Solihull U16s 1 – Wild Academy U16s 9

The Wild Academy Under 16 team came away from the West Midlands with an impressive 1-9 victory over Solihull U16s on Sunday.

Widnes took the lead on 3 minutes with a goal from Jaxon Kirk – Jones and the advantage was doubled just 2 minutes later with a strike from Liam Yarwood.

Solihull scored what would turn out to be their only goal of the game on 8 minutes but two goals within 21 seconds of each other – from Cody Ogden and Adam Vigh-Yecsey – and then a second for Yarwood gave the Wild a clear 1-5 lead at the first break.

There was only one goal in the second period – from Cody Ogden to make the score 1-6 to Widnes – but third period strikes saw Ogden and Yarwood both complete hat tricks and Vigh-Yecsey also scored a second.

12th March: Wild Academy U16s 11 – Grimsby U16s 2

The Wild Academy Under 16 team beat Grimsby U16s 11-2 at Planet Ice Widnes on Saturday.

Luke Alston fired the home side into the lead after just 7 seconds and further goals from Jared Knowles (2), Cody Ogden and Thomas Warburton saw Widnes lead 5-0 at the first period break.

Porter Harrop edged the Wild further ahead 70 seconds from the restart but then two quick goals for Grimsby gave the visitors a faint light of hope.

A third goal for Knowles just 25 seconds later gave him his hat trick and Warburton's second on 23 minutes gave the Wild a healthy 8-2 lead after two periods.

Further goals in the third period from Ogden, Jaxon Kirk Jones and Liam Yarwood rounded off the scoring for the match and handed Widnes a comprehensive 11-2 victory.

2nd April 2022: Wild Academy U16s 4 - Sutton U16s 1

The Wild Academy Under 16 team beat Sutton Under 16s 4-1 in a league game at Planet Ice Widnes on Saturday.

Sutton took the lead after just 65 seconds of the game but Widnes hit back with a goal from Cody Ogden on 13 minutes and the score remained 1-1 at the first period break.

Second period goals from Jaxon Kirk-Jones and Liam Yarwood put Widnes into the lead and a third period strike from Harrison Lightfoot rounded off the scoring for a 4-1 victory.

9th April: Sutton U16s 3 - Wild Academy U16s 10

The Wild Academy Under 16 team picked up their 4th win in a row with a comprehensive 3-10 win away at Sutton on Saturday.

Thomas Warburton opened the scoring for Widnes after 4 minutes, Sutton equalised but further goals from Cody Ogden, Harrison Lightfoot and Jaxon Kirk-Jones gave the Wild a healthy lead. Sutton pulled another goal back on 13 minutes but the score remained 2-4 for Widnes at the first period break.

Luke Alston edged the Wild further ahead early in the second period but this strike was countered by what would turn out to be Sutton's last goal of the game.

Two more goals came for Widnes – from Liam Yarwood, just 30 seconds apart, – and he completed his hat-trick with a third early in the third period.

Second goals for both Lightfoot and Ogden rounded off the scoring for the Wild and the win sees them remain in second place in the league table with one game left to play in the regular season.

23rd April: Manchester Storm U16s 1 – Wild Academy U16s 5

The Wild Academy Under 16 team finished off their regular league season with an impressive 1-5 victory away over Manchester Storm on Saturday.

Widnes took the lead after 9 minutes with a goal from Jared Knowles and a strike from Cody Ogden two minutes later saw them leading 0-2 at the first break. Jaxon Kirk Jones edged the Wild youngsters further ahead early in the second period but it took until the 34th minute for the hosts to find the back of the net themselves.

The Wild scored again just 30 seconds later with another from Cody Ogden and he completed his hat-trick with another strike in the 42nd minute.

The resulting 1-5 win means that Widnes finish the league campaign in 3rd place in the Under 16 table, behind unbeaten leaders Leeds and second place Sheffield.

24th April: Wild Academy U16s 5 – Leeds Knights U16s 5

The Wild Academy Under 16 team picked up a creditable draw with league leaders Leeds Knights Under 16s in a challenge match at Planet Ice Widnes on Sunday.

The Knights have won all of their league games this season – including home and away victories over Widnes - so this was a superb achievement, especially with the Wild youngsters having already played a tough game away in Manchester the day before.

This game was closely fought throughout, very entertaining to watch and the end result remained until the very last second.

Widnes took the lead on 3 minutes through Aidan Lamb but Leeds equalised 30 seconds later and then went ahead themselves on 7 minutes. A 9th minute equaliser from Luke Alston – short handed – put the teams back on level terms and the score remained 2-2 at the first break.

The Wild retook the lead briefly in the second period with a goal from Liam Yarwood but that was cancelled out by a Leeds counter and the match remained on a knife edge at 3-3 heading into the final period.

Leeds sneaked back into the lead just 76 seconds from the restart but Widnes equalised again with a second goal from Yarwood just 80 seconds later.

A powerplay goal from Yarwood – to complete his hat-trick – on 34 minutes put the Wild back in front but another strike from Leeds tied the game up at 5-5.

The two teams will meet again in the return match away in Yorkshire on Saturday 7th May

7th May: Leeds U16s 6 – Wild Academy U16s 1

The Wild Academy Under 16 team missed out on the chance of winning this post-season challenge series against league champions Leeds after they lost out 6-1 away in Yorkshire on Saturday.

Honours had been even in the home and away challenge after a 5-5 draw back in Widnes two weeks earlier and the Wild U16s, who have just finished the season in a highly creditable third place in the league were hoping to come home with a result against the hitherto unbeaten team.

Unfortunately, as it turned out, the match followed league form and Leeds ended up easy winners.

Widnes put up a good fight, however, and it took until the 10th minute of the game for the initial deadlock to be broken.

Unfortunately, Leeds scored two quick goals just 45 seconds apart and took a 2-0 lead into the first period break.

Two more unanswered Leeds goals followed in the second period but Widnes finally broke their duck at the start of the third with a strike from Cody Ogden on 32 minutes.

Any hopes of a late Wild comeback were dashed, however, as Leeds scored again 3 minutes later and added their 6th and final goal on 43 minutes.

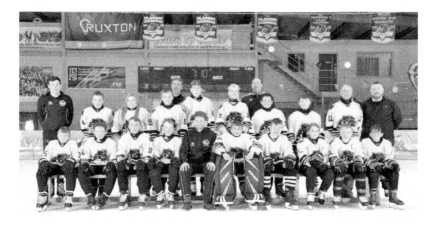

Widnes Wild Academy Under 14 Team Photo – Season 2021/22
(Photo by Geoff White)

WILD ACADEMY UNDER 14 SEASON REVIEW

The Wild Academy Under 14 team enjoyed a successful season in the highly competitive 10-team Under 14 North Division 2, finishing in 4th place overall.

They won 10 of their 18 league games finishing ahead of long established junior teams such as Sheffield, Solihull, Manchester Storm and Blackburn and just 2 points behind 3rd placed Sutton – who have an awesome reputation for developing young players.

Aside from heavy home and away defeats against the top two teams - Leeds and Kingston - Widnes were never outplayed and, in their four meetings with Sutton over the course of the season (two league and two challenge matches), the results could easily have gone either way on each occasion.

The top points scorer was Jared Knowles with 37 goals and 12 assists from 18 league games and he finished up 4th in the overall league standings. Aidan Lamb was second highest points scorer for Widnes with 16 + 19 and he finished 7th overall

Austin Busby and Sophia Green also made it into double figures in terms of league points - with 4+9 and 8+5 respectively - and Alexandra Vigh Yecsey joined them in double digits for the season with 2 goals in challenge games to add to her 2+6 in the league.

Jared Knowles (above - #19) and Aidan Lamb (below – # 11) were the leading scorers for the Wild Academy Under 14 team in the 2021/22 Season. Both also made appearances for the Widnes U16 team. (Photos by Geoff White)

Final League Table Under 14N2 – Season 2021/22

	P	W	D	L	F	A	+/-	PIM	Pts
Leeds Jr Knights	18	17	1	0	183	7	176	28	35
Kingston	18	15	1	2	152	25	127	113	31
Sutton	18	11	1	6	87	84	3	147	23
Widnes Wild	18	10	1	7	85	84	1	58	21
Sheffield	18	8	2	8	86	79	7	62	18
Solihull	18	6	3	9	79	95	-16	46	15
Manchester Storm	18	7	0	11	61	90	-29	79	14
Blackburn	18	5	1	12	56	115	-59	112	11
Billingham Stars	18	4	2	12	59	134	-75	74	10
Coventry	18	1	0	17	32	167	-135	44	2

Top Points Scorers

Player	Team	GP	G	A	Pts	PIM
Beau Reader	Kingston	16	48	26	74	69
Charlie Powell	Kingston	15	34	25	59	4
Dylan Smith	Kingston	16	27	27	54	0
Jared Knowles	Widnes Wild	18	37	12	49	6
Felix Sorensen	Kingston	15	20	22	42	4
Jake Wigginton	Leeds Jr Knights	12	19	19	38	0
Aidan Lamb	Widnes Wild	16	16	19	35	2
Edgars Vengis	Leeds Jr Knights	12	21	14	35	2

Top Netminders

Netminder	Team	GPI	SA	GA	SA%	SO
Harrison Mccourt	Leeds Jr	12	109	7	93.58%	8
Jacob Mardell	Blackburn	6	352	40	88.64%	0
Lewis Hulks	Kingston	16	148	17	88.51%	8
Lewis Hulks	Blackburn	1	148	17	88.51%	8
Harrie Fairfax	Solihull	10	151	19	87.42%	1
Emily Johnson	Kingston	15	90	12	86.67%	7
Finn Wilson	Sheffield	11	190	30	84.21%	3
Finn Ogden	Widnes Wild	18	494	84	83.00%	1

Wild Academy Under 14 Team Player Statistics
Season 2021/22

Player	U14 League				Challenge		Totals				PIM
	GP	G	A	Pts	GP	Pts	GP	G	A	Pts	
Jared Knowles	18	37	12	49	3	8	21	42	15	57	6
Aidan Lamb	16	16	19	35	3	9	19	21	23	44	2
Austin Busby	18	4	9	13	3	1	21	5	9	14	0
Sophia Green	17	8	5	13	2	0	19	8	5	13	6
Alexandra V-Yecsey	16	2	6	8	3	2	19	4	6	10	2
Reece O'Brien	14	5	2	7	2	0	16	5	2	7	4
Evan Walker	11	6	0	6	0	0	11	6	0	6	0
Ruben Price	10	2	3	5	1	0	11	2	3	5	6
Callum Sweeney	15	3	1	4	2	0	17	3	1	4	10
Morgan Busby	18	0	3	3	3	1	21	0	4	4	6
Lewis Speare	16	1	2	3	3	1	19	1	3	4	0
Daniel Stephens	15	1	2	3	3	0	18	1	2	3	0
Alex Reid	5	0	0	0	2	2	7	0	2	2	0
Jack Daniel Ross	6	0	1	1	2	0	8	0	1	1	0
Alfred Shearn	2	0	1	1	0	0	2	0	1	1	0
Charles Shearn	16	0	1	1	3	0	19	0	1	1	12
John Lamb	12	0	0	0	1	0	13	0	0	0	2
Mark Norman	13	0	0	0	3	0	16	0	0	0	2
Finn Ogden	18	0	0	0	3	0	21	0	0	0	0
Roberts Ziraks	8	0	0	0	3	0	11	0	0	0	0

Netminder		GPI	SA	GA	Sv%	SO
Finn Ogden	League	18	494	84	83.00%	1
	Chall	3	86	14	83.72%	0
	Total	21	580	98	**83.10%**	1

Finn Ogden was an ever-present in the U14s net, playing in all 21 league and challenge games for an overall Sa% of 83.10 (Photo by Geoff White)

Wild Academy Under 14 Team

Fixtures & Results – Season 2021/22

Date	Game	Home	Score	Score	Away	WDL
26/09/2021	U14N2	Sheffield	4	5	Widnes	W
02/10/2021	U14N2	Leeds	12	0	Widnes	L
09/10/2021	U14N2	Widnes	4	3	Mcr Storm	W
23/10/2021	U14N2	Widnes	11	0	Blackburn	W
20/11/2021	U14N2	Widnes	1	13	Leeds	L
27/11/2021	U14N2	Widnes	0	2	Sutton	L
04/12/2021	U14N2	Widnes	1	10	Kingston	L
11/12/2021	U14N2	Blackburn	1	3	Widnes	W
08/01/2022	U14N2	Widnes	9	2	Sheffield	W
15/01/2022	U14N2	Mcr Storm	4	2	Widnes	L
29/01/2022	U14N2	Widnes	6	1	Coventry	W
12/02/2022	U14N2	Kingston	8	0	Widnes	L
26/02/2022	U14N2	Billingham	4	7	Widnes	W
05/03/2022	U14N2	Widnes	10	1	Billingham	W
19/03/2022	Chall	Widnes	2	3	Mcr Storm	L
20/03/2022	U14N2	Coventry	2	11	Widnes	W
26/03/2022	Chall	Sutton	6	4	Widnes	L
02/04/2022	Chall	Widnes	6	5	Sutton	W
09/04/2022	U14N2	Sutton	8	5	Widnes	L
30/04/2022	U14N2	Widnes	6	5	Solihull	W
01/05/2022	U14N2	Solihull	4	4	Widnes	D

Wild Academy Under 14 Team Match Reports

26th September: Sheffield U14s 4 - Wild Academy U14s 5

The Wild Academy Under 14 team picked up a superb last ditch 4-5 away win over the highly rated Sheffield juniors at iceSheffield on Sunday.

Widnes took the lead with a goal from team captain Aidan Lamb after just 23 seconds and the score remained 0-1 at the first period break. Sheffield scored twice early in the second period to take the lead but a second strike from Lamb levelled again on 29 minutes.

Sheffield edged ahead again with a 3rd goal just 30 seconds into the third period but Lamb's hat trick goal just 30 seconds after that tied the game once more.

This was a highly entertaining and evenly fought game throughout and Sheffield took the lead again on 36 minutes only for Widnes to equalise once more with a debut Wild goal for Sophia Green.

With time ticking away and a draw looking the likely result, Sheffield removed their netminder for the last minute in favour of an extra attacker but the move backfired and Widnes secured the win with an empty net goal from Jared Knowles just 18 seconds from time.

Finn Ogden put in a superb performance in goal for the Wild, turning away 18 of the 22 shots that he faced.

2nd October: Leeds U14s 12 – Wild Academy U14s 0

The Wild Academy Under 14 team suffered a heavy 12-0 defeat away to the Leeds U14s on Saturday, in what was the first ever league game for the Yorkshire side.

The Wild team featured several younger players who were "playing up" at a level higher then their usual age group and were up against it right from the start. Leeds scored after just 70 seconds of the game and went 2-0 up 27 seconds later. The score was 7-0 to the hosts at the end of the first period and they reached the 12-0 cut off point in the 23rd minute of the game.

Under junior league rules to avoid one-sided scorelines, once a team gets 12 goals ahead in a match, no further scoring is recorded and the remaining game time is played out for fun.

9th October: Wild Academy U14s 4 – Manchester Storm U14s 3

The Wild Academy Under 14 team picked up a superb 4-3 win over the Manchester Storm U14s at Planet Ice Widnes on Saturday.

Manchester actually scored first on 9 minutes but an equaliser from Jared Knowles saw the score level at the first period break.

Two second periods goals – from Austin Busby and Knowles again – saw the Wild edge further ahead and a goal right at the start of the third period from Alexandra Vigh-Yecsey made it 4-1 to Widnes.

A 32nd minute goal for Manchester narrowed the gap and then a third strike on 38 minutes left the game on a knife edge. Widnes defended well, however and held on for the win.

They are now level on points with league leaders Leeds at this early stage of the season.

23rd October: Wild Academy U14s 11 – Blackburn U14s 0

The Wild Academy Under 14 team beat Blackburn Under 14s 11-0 at Planet Ice Widnes on Saturday.

Sophia Green opened the scoring for the Wild on 5 minutes and team captain Aidan Lamb made it 2-0 just 90 seconds later. The score remained 2-0 at the first period break but Widnes edged further ahead with a powerplay goal from Austin Busby on 29 minutes to lead 3-0 at the end of the second period.

What had been a fairly close game turned into a rout in the third period as Widnes scored 8 more unanswered goals – with 4 from Jared Knowles, 3 more from Lamb and 1 from Alexandra Vigh-Yecsey.

Finn Ogden put in a solid performance in the Wild net recording a shut-out, although he did only have 11 shots to face over the course of the game – but needed to maintain concentration during long periods of inactivity.

The win sees the Widnes youngsters remain in second place in the league table, level on points with leaders Leeds but having played a game more.

20th November: Wild Academy U14s 1 – Leeds U14s 13

The Wild Academy Under 14 team took on the Leeds U14 team at Planet Ice Widnes on Saturday, slumping to a 1-13 defeat.

Leeds are the current league leaders and they arrived on Merseyside with a perfect 100% record for their 4 games to date, during which they hadn't conceded a single goal.

The visitors took the lead in the 5th minute and had added 5 more by the time Widnes found the back of the net with a strike from Sophia Green.

The score remained 1-6 at first period break but 6 more unanswered goals for Leeds in the second period put the game well beyond the reach of the Widnes youngsters.

Leeds took the foot off the pedal somewhat in the third period and the game finished up 1-13 but, despite the defeat, the Wild U14s can, at least, take the credit for scoring the first competitive goal against Leeds this season.

27th November: Wild Academy U14s 0 – Sutton U14s 2

The Wild Academy Under 14 team lost 0-2 at home to Sutton U14s at Planet Ice Widnes on Saturday.

This was a very close game throughout and a good performance by the Widnes team - which featured several under-age players who were playing up a level – against a very experienced Sutton side.

The visitors took the lead after just 35 seconds of the game and the score remained 0-1 at the first period break. A second goal doubled the lead on 20 minutes and that rounded off the scoring for the game.

The Wild Under 14s are next in action this Saturday when they play Kingston (Hull) U14s at Planet Ice Widnes – 4.50pm face off.

4th December: Wild Academy U14s 1 – Kingston U14s 10

The Wild Academy Under 14 team lost 1-10 to a very strong and experienced Kingston (Hull) U14 team at Planet Ice Widnes on Saturday.

The visitors opened the scoring in the 3rd minute and were 0-6 up by the first period break. Such was the domination of the Hull side that Widnes didn't manage a single shot on goal in the first period – and only 2 in the second during which time the Humbersiders scored two more unanswered goals to lead 0-8.

The score was 0-9 before Widnes finally found the back of the net - with a goal from team captain Aidan Lamb in the 36th minute – and Hull rounded off the scoring 5 minutes later to take the 1-10 victory.

11th December: Blackburn U14s 1 – Wild Academy U14s 3

The Wild Academy Under 14 team moved up to third place in the league table after a 1-3 win away to Blackburn on Saturday.

This was a very entertaining game to watch and could have gone either way. Widnes took the lead with just 30 seconds left to go in the first period with a short handed goal from Jared Knowles.

Blackburn equalised early in the second period but the game was decided by two quick fire goals just 30 seconds apart on 19 minutes from Knowles again and Sophia Green to give Widnes a 1-3 lead.

The remaining 26 minutes remained goal-less with Finn Ogden putting in a good performance in the Wild net.

8th January – Wild Academy Under 14s 9 – Sheffield Under 14s 2

The Wild Academy Under 14 team moved up to second in the league table with a 9-2 win over Sheffield Under 14s at Planet Ice Widnes on Saturday.

Widnes took the lead with a Jared Knowles goal on 3 minutes, Sheffield equalised on 10 minutes but further strikes from Reece O'Brien and Lewis Speare saw the Wild leading 3-1 at the end of the first period.

The second period saw just one goal – from Evan Walker, one of several U12 players who was playing up a level for this game. Sheffield scored first in the third period but Walker scored again and this was followed by a three from Knowles and a hat-trick strike from Walker to hand Widnes an important victory over the Steel City team.

The Wild Academy Under 14 team are now level on points with league leaders Leeds U14s, although they have played more games.

15th January 2022 – Mcr Storm U14s 4 – Wild Academy U14s 2

The Wild Academy Under 14 team lost 4-2 away to Manchester Storm Under 14s on Saturday.

Manchester took the lead in the 5th minute but Widnes equalised on 10 minutes with a goal from Jared Knowles. Two more goals followed for the hosts on either side of the first period break and a

4th on 28 minutes gave them a commanding lead heading into the final period.

A second strike for Knowles on 39 minutes narrowed the deficit but that was the last goal of the game and Manchester held on for the win.

29th January 2022: Wild Academy U14s 6 – Coventry U14s 1

The Wild Academy Under 14 team continued their superb run of results with a 6-1 win over bottom team Coventry U14s at Planet Ice Widnes on Saturday.

Widnes led 2-0 at the first break though goals from Aidan Lamb and Jared Knowles and 3 more strikes in the second period – from Lamb, Callum Sweeney and Ruben Price saw then well in the lead.

Knowles scored again early in the third period to put Widnes 6-0 up and then Coventry scored their only goal of the game on 38 minutes to round off the scoring.

12th February: Kingston U14s 8 – Wild Academy U14s 0

The Wild Academy Under 14 team lost 8-0 away to Kingston (Hull) U14s on Saturday.

It was an uncharacteristically below-par performance for the Wild youngsters compared to recent weeks and the home side took the lead after just 15 seconds.

By the end of the first period the score was 5-0 to Kingston and at the end of the second it was 6-0. Two more unanswered goals in the third period rounded off the scoring for the game.

Following this result, Kingston leapfrog Widnes into second place in the league table. Both teams have 12 points but the Hull side have the better playing record and have played fewer games.

26th February 2022: Billingham U14s 4 – Wild Academy U14s 7

The Wild Academy Under 14 team made it a double whammy for Widnes after they emulated their U12 team mates to win 4-7 away at Billingham Stars U12s on Saturday.

The hosts opened the scoring after just 2 minutes of the game and led 2-0 by the first period break.

Evan Walker – playing his second game of the day and stepping up from his usual age level - pulled a goal back for the Wild 3 minutes from the restart and two more goals, from Reece O'Brien and Jared Knowles, had Widnes leading 2-3 at the end of the second period.

They continued the third period in similar vein and a second goal from O'Brien after just 24 seconds put the Wild youngsters well and truly in the driving seat. A second goal for Knowles less than a minute later put Widnes 2-5 up but Billingham pulled a goal back on 38 minutes.

A Ruben Price strike restored the 3-goal advantage for Widnes but that was countered by another Billingham goal - and then, with just 24 seconds left on the clock, Reece O'Brien rounded off his hat trick with a 7th – and final goal - for the Wild.

5th March: Wild Academy U14s 10 – Billingham Star U14s 1

The Wild Academy Under 14 team put in a superb performance to beat Billingham 10-1 at Planet Ice Widnes on Saturday.

After a tense opening phase Widnes took the lead on 11 minutes through Jared Knowles and the score remained 1-0 at the first period break.

Second period goals from Knowles again, Evan Walker and Sophia Green gave the Wild youngsters a 4-0 lead before Billingham scored their only goal of the game on 28 minutes. A strike by Callum Sweeney just 60 seconds later gave Widnes a 5-1 lead at the end of second period.

Five unanswered goals for Widnes in the third period – from Reece O'Brien, Green again and three more for Jared Knowles for an impressive 5 overall in the game - saw the Wild Academy cruise to a convincing 10-1 win over the north east visitors and they remain in third place in the league table as a result.

19th March: Widnes U14s 2 – Manchester Storm U14 3

The Wild Academy lost 2-3 at home to Manchester Storm in a challenge game at Planet Ice Widnes on Saturday.

Widnes opened the scoring on 11 minutes with a goal from Jared Knowles and 21-0 at the first break. Manchester scored two quick goals to take the lead early in the second period and a third goal at the start of the third put them 1-3 ahead.

A second goal for Knowles with just 20 seconds left in the game came too late to spark a Widnes revival.

20th March: Coventry U14s 2 - Wild Academy U14s 11

The Wild Academy Under 14 team beat Coventry 2-11 away in the Midlands on Sunday.

Coventry took the lead after just 40 seconds of the game but a goal from Jared Knowles on 9 minutes levelled the score.

Three second period goals - from Callum Sweeney, Aidan Lamb and Sophie Green – fired the Wild into a commanding lead and despite conceding a second goal on 24 minutes, they never really looked like losing from this point on.

Knowles edged the Wild further ahead with his second goal of the game just 34 seconds into the third period and then hit two more goals within 20 seconds of each other to bring his tally for the game to 4.

Two more goals for Aidan Lamb, a 5th for Knowles and then a last ditch strike from Sophia Green with just 9 seconds left on the clock handed Widnes a convincing 2-11 win.

The day before, the Wild Under 14 team lost 2-3 to Manchester Storm U14s in a challenge match at Planet Ice Widnes.

Jared Knowles scored both goals in a game that saw Widnes outshoot the short benched visitors but they were unable to make the most of their chances.

The Wild Academy Under 14 team are away to Sutton U14s in a challenge game at the Lammas Road rink in Sutton-in-Ashfield on Saturday 26th March – 2.10pm face off. The return game will be played at Planet Ice Widnes on Saturday 2nd April – 3.20pm face off.

26th March 2022: Sutton U14s 6 – Wild Academy U14s 4

The Wild Academy Under 14 team lost 6-4 in a challenge match away to the Sutton U14s in their compact and bijou Lammas Road rink on Saturday.

Despite outshooting the opposition by 2 to 1 over the course of the game, they weren't able to take full advantage of their opportunities and went behind after 6 minutes.

Austin Busby drew the Wild youngsters level on 10 minutes but a further goal for the hosts gave them a 2-1 lead at the first period break.

Sutton edged further ahead just 1 minute into the second period but a goal from Jared Knowles on 27 minutes ensured that Widnes remained in touching distance heading into the third and final period.

Sutton scored again right at the start of the third and, once again, Widnes countered with a strike from Alexandra Vigh-Yecsey just 60 seconds later. The same thing happened again two minutes later with another Sutton goal and a Widnes counter from Vigh-Yecsey just 11 seconds apart but, try as they might, the Wild youngsters were unable to get that extra breakthrough to take control of the game.

A later strike for the hosts on 43 minutes rounded off the scoring for the match and gave them a narrow 6-4 victory.

The two teams will meet again in the return match at Planet Ice Widnes this Saturday 2nd April, 3.20pm face off

2nd April 2022: Wild Academy U14s 6 - Sutton U14s 5

The Wild Academy Under 14 team beat Sutton Under 14s 6-5 in a highly entertaining challenge game at Planet Ice Widnes on Saturday.

Sutton took the lead after just 34 seconds of the game and went 0-2 up on 3 minutes but goals from Aidan Lamb and Jared Knowles saw Widnes draw level.

Two more goals late in the period gave the visitors a clear lead heading into the first break and they went 2-5 up with a further goal in the 22nd minute.

The Wild youngsters upped their game after this and Aidan Lamb pulled a goal back within 60 seconds. A hat-trick goal for Lamb with just 40 seconds left in the period brought the score to 4-5.

Two more unanswered goals – a fourth for Lamb and a second for Knowles – propelled the Wild into the lead in the third period and they held on for a 6-5 win.

Saturday 9th April: Sutton U14s 8- Wild Academy U14s 5

The Wild Academy Under 14 team lost 8-5 away to Sutton U14s on Saturday.

While they gave a good account of themselves overall, goals from Jared Knowles (2), Daniel Stephens (his first for the club), Austin Busby and Aidan Lamb were not enough to stave off defeat and the Wild remain in a three-way battle for third place in the league table with two games left to play.

30th April: Wild Academy U14s 6 – Solihull U14s 5

The Wild Academy Under 14 team picked up a crucial 6-5 win over Solihull U14s at Planet Ice on Saturday.

Widnes are locked in 2-way battle with Sutton U14s to finish in 3rd place in the Under 14 league table and, at this final stage of the season, every point is vital.

The Wild took the lead after just 70 seconds of the game with a goal from captain Aidan Lamb and a goal from Austin Busby on 5 minutes saw them edge further ahead. Solihull struck back but a goal from Evan Walker on 10 minutes saw Widnes lead 3-1 at the first period break.

Two goals early in the second period saw Solihull draw level but Widnes took the lead once again – through Jared Knowles on 26 minutes, only to see Solihull equalise once more just 40 seconds later.

A second goal for Lamb early in the third period saw Widnes edge back in front again but that was also countered by a further Solihull goal. The game was finally decided by a second goal of the night for Jared Knowles with just over 70 seconds left on the clock.

1st May: Solihull U14s 4 – Wild Academy U14s 4

The Wild Academy Under 14 team rounded off their league season with a 4-4 draw away to Solihull Under 14s.

The same two teams had met the week before in a highly entertaining and closely matched game, which ended in a 6-5 win for Widnes, and this meeting was expected to be similarly competitive.

Solihull took the lead on 7 minutes but Widnes hit back with a strike from Jared Knowles 4 minutes later and the score remained 1-1 at the first period break.

The hosts scored again just 33 seconds from the restart to edge back into the lead but Widnes equalised once more with a second goal from Knowles on 23 minutes. The same player then scored his hat–trick goal just 11 seconds from the buzzer to give Widnes a 2-3 lead at the second break.

Continuing what had been a see-sawing game from the very start, Solihull drew level again with a goal just 36 seconds into the third period but Knowles fired Widnes back into the lead with his 4th goal of the game 52 seconds later.

Widnes had the upper hand for much of the third period – outshooting Solihull by 13 to 8 - but they weren't able to further extend their lead. The hosts fought back to score a "game tying goal" on 40 minutes and the score remained 4-4 at the final buzzer.

The Wild youngsters finish in 4th place in the 10-team Under 14 league table with 21 points from 18 games.

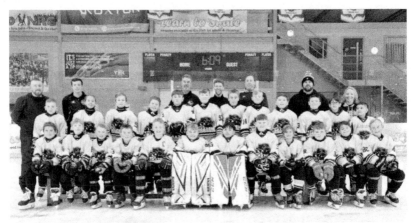

Widnes Wild Academy Under 12 and Under 10 Combined Team Photo – Season 2021/22 (Photo by Geoff White)

WILD ACADEMY UNDER 12 SEASON REVIEW

The Wild Academy Under 12 team had an entertaining season in the 8 team Under 12 North Division, finishing a very creditable 5th over all.

Playing as the Under 11s under the previous system - and relying heavily on the use of under-age players to maintain numbers - the team had failed to win a single game in their debut 2019/20 season and they had to wait until December this season to notch up their first ever win with a victory away at Blackburn.

But then, the home defeat to Manchester in the first game of the season was overturned and awarded as a 5-0 forfeit after the Storm had iced a short bench, so the Wild U12s finished the calendar year with two wins under their belts.

Things improved in the second half of the season as the team continued to gel and they managed 4 more wins to top off their best ever season to date.

The leading points scorer for the season was Jacob Foster – formerly of Deeside Dragons - with 9 goals and 1 assist from 11 league and challenge matches.

Final League Table Under 12N – Season 2021/22

	P	W	D	L	F	A	+/-	PIM	Pts
Bradford	14	13	1	0	103	13	90	108	27
Leeds Jr Knights	14	9	2	3	78	30	48	38	19*
Whitley Bay	14	8	2	4	76	55	21	54	18
Manchester Storm	14	6	3	5	77	58	19	16	14*
Widnes Wild	14	6	1	7	44	66	-22	56	13
Blackburn	14	5	1	8	39	73	-34	20	11
Kingston	14	3	0	11	50	89	-39	54	4*
Billingham Stars	14	0	2	12	6	89	-83	14	0*

Top Points Scorers

Player	Team	GP	G	A	Pts	PIM
Evan Bradon	Leeds Jr Knights	11	19	18	37	6
Christian Roth	Manchester Storm	11	21	9	30	2
Kyle Bower	Bradford	12	24	5	29	4
Mario Vaksmansky	Manchester Storm	7	18	10	28	2
Zach Taylor	Leeds Jr Knights	13	15	10	25	0

Top Netminders

Player	Team	GP	SA	GA	Sv%	SO
Jacob Mardell	Bradford	13	256	15	94.14%	7
Harrison Mccourt	Leeds Jr Knights	8	70	9	87.14%	4
Mason Harling	Leeds Jr Knights	12	90	12	86.67%	5
Ansel Groot	Whitley Bay	9	134	18	86.57%	2
Mason Holding	Manchester Storm	8	87	12	86.21%	3

(continued from previous page...)

Evan Walker matched his tally in the league of 8+1. Ruben Price weighed in with the most assists for the season – with 5.

Walker, Alfred Shearn and Miks Kirstens played in all 13 league games that were played (the away game at Whitley was awarded as an unplayed draw) and Kirstens and Chun Hei Kan shared netminding duties over the course of the season.

WILD ACADEMY UNDER 12 TEAM
Fixtures & Results – Season 2021/22

Date	Game	Home	Score	Score	Away	WDL
25/09/2021	U12N	Widnes	5	0	Mcr Storm	W a
09/10/2021	U12N	Widnes	4	12	Whitley Bay	L
16/10/2021	U12N	Mcr Storm	8	0	Widnes	L
27/11/2021	U12N	Widnes	0	6	Leeds	L
04/12/2021	U12N	Widnes	0	8	Bradford	L
18/12/2021	U12N	Blackburn	2	6	Widnes	W
29/01/2022	U12N	Leeds	8	0	Widnes	L
05/02/2022	U12N	Widnes	9	1	Blackburn	W
26/02/2022	U12N	Billingham	2	3	Widnes	W
05/03/2022	U12N	Widnes	9	3	Kingston	W
12/03/2022	U12N	Kingston	8	0	Widnes	L
23/04/2022	U12N	Bradford	8	0	Widnes	L
30/04/2022	U12N	Widnes	8	0	Billingham	W
10/05/2022	U12N	Whitley Bay	0	0	Widnes	D a
21/05/2022	CH	Whitley Bay	10	2	Widnes	L

Evan Walker (#2) leads the attack in a Wild Academy match against Bradford. Like several of his U12s team-mates, Walker played "up" a level for the U14s as well for his own age group this season and now has 38 career matches under his belt. (Photo by Hannah Walker)

WILD ACADEMY UNDER 12 TEAM

Player Statistics – Season 2021/22

Player	U12N League					Challenge				
	GP	G	A	Pts	PIM	GP	G	A	Pts	PIM
Jacob Foster	10	8	1	9	0	1	1	0	1	0
Evan Walker	13	8	1	9	4	0	0	0	0	0
Ruben Price	7	3	5	8	6	0	0	0	0	0
Caleb Eddleston	11	5	1	6	10	1	0	0	0	0
Ollie Cliffe	11	5	0	5	0	1	0	0	0	0
Leighton Williams	9	4	0	4	0	0	0	0	0	0
Max Goodey	9	2	1	3	0	1	0	0	0	0
Ben Roberts	9	3	0	3	0	1	0	0	0	0
Herbie Rolt	8	3	0	3	8	1	0	0	0	0
George Wakefield	9	2	1	3	4	1	0	0	0	0
Elias Boardman	3	0	1	1	0	0	0	0	0	0
Daniel Botes	10	0	1	1	0	0	0	0	0	0
Andrew Craciunescu	7	1	0	1	2	0	0	0	0	0
Alfred Shearn	13	0	1	1	2	1	0	0	0	0
Joel Babu	1	0	0	0	0	0	0	0	0	0
James Back	1	0	0	0	0	0	0	0	0	0
Lana Botes	10	0	0	0	4	0	0	0	0	0
Chun Hei Kan	10	0	0	0	0	1	0	0	0	0
Miks Kirsteins	13	0	0	0	0	1	0	0	0	0
John Lamb	11	0	0	0	0	1	0	0	0	0
Rhys Liversage	4	0	0	0	0	0	0	0	0	0
Ethan Liversage	12	0	0	0	6	1	0	0	0	2
Joseph Mason	10	0	0	0	2	1	0	0	0	0
Mark Norman	11	0	0	0	6	1	0	0	0	0
Milo Ogden	4	0	0	0	0	0	0	0	0	0
Heiko Petrusevicius	2	0	0	0	0	1	0	0	0	0
Ben Roberts	1	0	0	0	0	0	0	0	0	0
Stanley Shearn	3	0	0	0	0	1	1	0	1	0
Poppy Ward	1	0	0	0	2	0	0	0	0	0
Daniel Woods	4	0	0	0	2	1	0	0	0	0

Netminder	U12N League					Challenge			
	GP	SA	GA	SA%	SO	GP	SA	GA	SA%
Chun Hei Kan	10	96	23	76.04%	2	1	20	4	80.00%
Miks Kirsteins	13	200	53	73.50%	0	1	19	6	68.42%

WILD ACADEMY UNDER 12 TEAM
Match Reports – Season 2021/22

25th September: Wild Academy U12s 3 - Mcr Storm U12s 10

The Wild Academy Under 12 team lost 3-10 at home to the Manchester Storm U12s in their opening fixture of the new season at Planet Ice Widnes on Saturday.

The Storm took the lead after just 24 seconds of the match but two goals from Widnes' Caleb Eddlestone put the home team in front.

The Storm then scored twice more to lead 2-3 at the first period break. Three unanswered goals saw Manchester draw further ahead in the second period and they were 2-9 up by the time Ollie Cliffe fired in a third for Widnes.

A late goal for Manchester edged them into double figures but the Wild youngsters came away with lots of positives to build on.

The netminding duties for the Wild were shared by Chun Hei Kan and Miks Kersteins who turned away 32 of the 42 shots they faced between them.

NOTE: The game was later awarded as a 5-0 win to Widnes as Manchester had a short bench.

9th October: Wild Academy U12s 4 – Whitley Bay U12s 12

The Wild Academy Under 12 team lost 4-12 at home to Whitley Bay U12s at Planet Ice Widnes on Saturday.

Whitley scored first in the 3rd minute but the Wild equalised on 12 minutes through Herbie Rolt - then a powerplay goal just 70 seconds later gave the league leaders a narrow 1-2 lead at the first period break.

Whitley extended their lead with two goals early in the second period but a strike from Ruben Price kept Widnes in contention. Two more goals edged Whitley further ahead – countered by a second of the game for Widnes from Rolt - but the North East team ended the period with a 3-7 lead.

4 unanswered goals for the visitors after the restart put the game beyond the reach of the Widnes youngsters but a goal from Jacob

Foster on 40 minutes gave the home fans something to cheer about before Whitley wrapped up the scoring with a 12th goal in the last minute of the game.

16th October 2021: Mcr Storm U12s 8 - Wild Academy U12s 0

The Wild Academy Under 12 team lost 8-0 away to league leaders Manchester Storm Under 12s in Altrincham on Saturday.

The Widnes Under 12 team has a number of under age players from the U10s in the side, who are able to gain invaluable experience of playing at a higher level.

Potential new players are always welcome to apply to join the Academy teams at all age groups and interested parties are invited to contact head coach Mike Gilbert on 0151 420 7930 in the first instance.

27th November: Wild Academy U12s 0 – Leeds U12s 6

The Wild Academy Under 12 team lost 0-6 at home to league leaders Leeds U12s at Planet Ice Widnes on Saturday.

Leeds took the lead after just 59 seconds of the game and the score was 0-2 by the first period break. Two more unanswered goals in the second period extended the lead and two more in the third made this a comprehensive victory for the Yorkshire side.

The Wild Under 12s are next in action this Saturday when they play Bradford U12s at Planet Ice Widnes – 3.20pm face off.

4th December: Wild Academy U12s 0 – Bradford U12s 8

The Wild Academy Under 12 team lost 0-8 to the Bradford U12 team at Planet Ice Widnes on Saturday.

Bradford took the lead after just 23 seconds of the game and led 0-5 by the end of the first period.

Widnes were not outplayed in this game by any means and held their own in terms of possession and shots on goal for sustained periods, but they were just unable to make the most of their opportunities.

Two more goals from Bradford in the second period and another in the third put the game out of the Wild's reach and the Widnes Under 12s remain bottom of the league table, still searching for their first win of the season.

18th December: Blackburn Under 12s 2 – Wild Academy U12s 6

The Wild Academy Under 12 team picked up their first ever league win a 2-6 victory away to Blackburn U12s on Saturday.

Widnes opened the scoring after just 46 seconds with a goal from Evan Walker but Blackburn equalised on 10 minutes.

Walker struck again on 13 minutes to hand the Wild a narrow 1-2 lead at the first period break and the same player completed a straight hat-trick with his third goal on 17 minutes.

The rest of the second period was goal-less but Ben Roberts further extended the Widnes lead on 32 minutes. Blackburn scored again two minutes later but a 4th goal for the Wild just 40 seconds after that - from Leighton Williams - put them well and truly in the driving seat.

A fourth goal for Evan Walker rounded off the scoring for the game and the Wild youngsters came away from East Lancashire with a 2-6 victory.

Following that win, the Wild Under 12s move up to 5th place in the league table. They now actually have two wins to their credit after their first game of the season – a 3-10 home loss at the hands of Manchester Storm U12s - was awarded to them after the visitors iced an under-strength team.

Curiously enough, league rules dictate that, in such circumstances, even if the weakened team wins the game, it has to be awarded as a 5-0 victory to the non –offending side.

29th January 2022: Leeds U12s 8 - Wild Academy U12s 0

The Wild Academy Under 12 team lost 8-0 away to league leaders Leeds U12s on Saturday.

The Widnes youngsters held their own for much of the first period but went behind to two late goals. 4 more goals for Leeds in the second period put them well in front and 2 more in the third rounded off the scoring for the match.

5th February 2022: Wild Academy U12s 9 – Blackburn U12s 1

The Wild Academy Under 12 team picked up their third win of the season with a comprehensive 9-1 victory over Blackburn U12s at Planet Ice Widnes on Saturday.

The Widnes youngsters dominated the game throughout and outshot the visitors by 50 to 8 over the course of the game.

Evan Walker opened the scoring for Widnes in the 5th minute but Blackburn equalised 4 minutes later.

Two goals within 30 seconds of each other - from Ben Roberts and Herbie Rolt then gave the Wild a 3-1 lead at the first period break.

A goal from Caleb Eddlestone just 33 seconds from the restart extended the Widnes lead and further strikes from Max Goodey (2), Jacob Foster, and a second for both Roberts and Eddleston saw the Academy youngsters cruise to an easy victory.

26th February 2022: Billingham U12s 2 – Wild Academy U12s 3

The Wild Academy Under 12 team came away from the North East with a superb 2-3 victory over Billingham Stars U12s on Saturday.

Billingham scored first after 12 minutes in an otherwise goal-less opening period and team captain Evan Walker equalised for Widnes 5 minutes into the second. The score remained locked at 1-1 at the end of that period but two goals - from Andrew Craciunescu (his first in Wild colours) and a great short handed effort from Ruben Price – midway through the third, put the Wild into an unassailable lead.

A strike from Billingham with 3 minutes left to play left the game somewhat on a knife-edge but was not enough to spark a late Stars revival and Widnes held on for the win.

5th March: Wild Academy U12s 9 – Kingston (Hull) U12s 3

The Wild Academy Under 12 team beat Kingston (Hull) U12s 9-3 in a highly entertaining game at Planet Ice Widnes on Saturday.

Kingston took the lead on 5 minutes but Widnes equalised with a goal from George Wakefield just 2 minutes later.

A strike from Jacob Foster just before the break handed the Wild a 2-1 lead and second period goals from Leighton Williams and Ollie Cliffe (2 each) further extended the advantage.

A second goal for Wakefield and a hat trick goal for Cliffe in the third period brought the Widnes tally to 8 before Kingston scored their second goal of the game on 40 minutes.

A late exchange saw Evan Walker add another goal for Widnes and Kingston pull one back before the clock finally ticked down to a comprehensive 9-3 win for the Wild youngsters.

12th March: Kingston U12s 2 - Wild Academy U12s 2

The Wild Academy Under 12 team drew 2-2 away to Kingston U12s in Hull on Saturday.

Team captain Evan Walker opened the scoring for Widnes on 12 minutes and the Wild led 0-1 at the first period break. Two quick goals for Kingston early in the second period saw them edge into the lead but an equaliser from Jacob Foster with just 80 seconds left in the game salvaged a point for the Academy youngsters.

The Wild Academy U14s are at home to Manchester Storm U14s this Saturday 19th March at Planet Ice Widnes - 3.20pm face off and straight after that, the Academy Under 18 team are at home to Sheffield U18s, 5pm start.

Admission is free to all Wild Academy home games at Planet Ice Widnes and spectators are encouraged to go along and support the stars of the future.

23rd April: Bradford U12s 8 – Wild Academy U12s 0

The Wild Academy Under 12 team lost 8-0 away to league leaders Bradford Under 12s on Saturday.

The Widnes youngsters are currently 5th in the league table with 2 games left to play. They are at home to Billingham this Saturday, 3.20pm face off.

30th April: Wild Academy Under 12s 8 – Billingham U12s 0

The Wild Academy Under 12 team picked up an impressive 8-0 shut out win over Billingham Under 12s at Planet Ice Widnes on Saturday.

Widnes took the lead after just 36 seconds with a goal from Caleb Eddleston and were leading 4-0 by the first period break courtesy of further strikes from Ollie Cliffe, Jacob Foster and Leighton Williams.

The Wild youngsters were clearly on top throughout this game and the onslaught continued in the second period with goals from Ruben Price and three more from Foster, to round off an impressive 4-goal haul.

The Widnes netminding pair of Miks Kersteins and Chun Hei Kan shared the goal-tending duties and managed to achieve the Under 12 team's first ever shut out performance.

10th May 2022: Whitley Bay U12s 0 – Wild Academy U12s 0

This game was not played and was assessed a 0-0 draw by the EIHA for the purposes of the league table.

21st May: Whitley Bay U12s 10 – Wild Academy U12s 2

The Wild Academy Under 12 team rounded off their season with a 10-2 challenge match defeat away to Whitley Bay on Saturday.

It was a very plucky performance by the Wild youngsters - who had a number of Under 10 age group players in their line up – particularly after an early start and long journey to the North East for the 12 noon face off.

Whitley took the lead just one minute into the game and built up a 3-0 by the time Widnes scored their first goal – through Stanley Shearn, with 30 seconds left in the period.

Three unanswered goals followed for the hosts and they led 6-1 at the second break and added two more early in the third period.

The Wild's second goal of the game eventually came on 38 minutes with a strike from Jacob Foster but two more goals for Whitley just 22 seconds apart quashed any hopes of a late Wild rally.

The Wild Academy Under 10 Team With the U10s Pool B Play Off Trophy
(Photo by Hannah Walker)

Wild Academy Under 10 Team Season Review
by Danny Cliffe, U10s Team Manager

The Under 10s season is made up of multiple days of "cross-ice" games held typically between the same teams throughout the year. This season the Widnes Wild Academy faced Manchester, Bradford, and Telford, and also guested once at Hull mid-way through the season.

Games are played across the width of the ice, instead of using the full length of it, and are played for fun with no scores being recorded or player statistics officially collected.

The Wild U10 team started the season with no goalie and, under an EIHA ruling, were allowed to play an U12 goalie in order to get the season going. However, midway through the season saw two goaltenders join the team and both started their journey with focus and determination.

Jacob Shaw and Henry Pearson both took turns in goal and also stood in for the opposition in the cross ice events to help other teams out who were missing their own goalie.

With both new and returning players to the U10s squad, the focus for the season has always been and will remain to have lots of fun.

Working as a team and concentrating on passing, shooting, finding space, learning positions and communicating between all of the players, helped the Wild Academy go from strength to strength as the season progressed.

Due to player shortages within the U12s team, many of the U10s were asked to play up an age group and each one has done themselves very proud.

The U10s built the philosophy of "B Y B" which means to "Be Your Best". Each player mentioned below did exactly that for the whole season, they played as best as they could regardless of opponent and came off every shift with a huge beaming smile!

The Wild Academy U10s players for season 2021/22 were:

Joel Babu, James Back, Augustin Balaz, Elias Boardman, Ollie Cliffe, Jacob Downe, Caleb Eddleston, Max Goodey, Rex Goodey, Ethan Liversage, Kian Liversage, Lilly Miller, Heiko Petrusevicius, Jacob Shaw, Stanley Shearn, Harrison Ward, Poppy Ward, Henry Pearson.

Sheffield Tournament 16th July 2022
Report By Danny Cliffe

The Widnes Wild Academy Under 10 team attended the EIHA's Sheffield tournament on Saturday 16th July and for many this was the first full day tournament that they had attended and played in games with recorded goals and win/loss points.

The team were set for a very long day with at least 7 games ahead of them and each member of the team made a commitment to each other to "B.Y.B" (Be Your Best).

Whilst the day started off slowly, the Widnes team went on to win every single game during the group stage including several games which hit the mercy ruling of +8 goals against their opponents.

After a very dominant display towards the end of the group stages the team were excited to learn they finished top of the group and went on to face Sheffield's own Mini-Samurais team.

The Wild youngsters comfortably won their semi-final and moved on to the final to face Milton Keynes Storm who had been the closest team to Widnes in the group stages.

The Wild Academy began the game with some nervousness but managed to find their rhythm once again and became the Pool B champions after a 5-3 win.

The tournament rounds off a very successful season for the U10s which consisted of only a single defeat all season.

The Wild Academy U10 team consisted of: Henry Pearson (netminder), Caleb Eddleston, Ollie Cliffe, Max Goodey, Ethan Liversage, Stanley Shearn, Jacob Shaw (netminder), James Back, Poppy Ward, Harrison Ward, Elias Boardman and Kian Liversage. Coaching staff: Danny Cliffe (Manager), Terry Gray (L2 Coach) and Gary Eddleston (L1 Coach).

The Wild Academy Under 10 team celebrating their trophy win on the ice at Sheffield
(Photo by Widnes Wild Academy)

Older age groups presenting an Academy jersey given as a thank you to announcer Colin Ellis for his dedication and support to the Academy all season.
(Photo by Hannah Walker)

Wild Academy End Of Season Awards

The end of season awards night for all the Academy junior teams was held at Widnes RUFC clubhouse and was attended by players, coaches, team staff, parents and other family members.

Along with various awards for particular players in each of the team age groups, they were two club-wide awards that were presented for the first time in memory of significant figures who have made an important contribution to ice hockey in Widnes.

The Vernon Neil award was presented in memory of the popular former rink manager at Planet Ice who sadly died in March 2022.

Vernon had been a key figure in the Silver Blades organisation that built and operated the Widnes rink before its merger with Planet Ice. He was rink manager at Widnes for a while and also had stints at Altrincham and Nottingham.

The inaugural Vernon Neil Hardworker Award was presented to Wild Academy Under 12 team player Ben Roberts.

The second award was dedicated in memory of Jon "Bo Bo" Little who was a popular coach at the Wild Junior Academy and who died in May 2020.

Jon played league ice hockey as netminder for the Trafford Metros at Altrincham and was a respected junior coach there for with the various Trafford, Phoenix and Manchester Storm teams.

He switched to Widnes in 2018 where he was an important member of the coaching staff and also bench coached a number of matches for the Wild Women's team and Widnes based recreational teams.

The recipient of the inaugural Jon Little Recognition Shield was Jake Meehan who plays for the Wild Academy Under 18 team and was also selected for the North Showcase U17 team this season.

The awards were presented by Wild Academy head coach Mike Gilbert, President Terry Gray, manager Danny Cliffe and, as a special gesture, Jon Little's partner Lynda Bird was called up onto the stage to present his shield to the first ever winner.

The award winners in each age group were as follows:

Under 10s
Players' Player Of The Season – Harrison Ward
Coaches' Player Of The Season – Caleb Eddleston
Most Improved Player – Kian Liversage

Under 12s
Players' Player Of The Season – Ant Norman
Coaches' Player Of The Season – Ben Roberts
Most Improved Player– Leighton Williams
Most Points For The Season – Jacob Foster
Unsung Hero – Kayton Kan

Under 14s
Players' Player Of The Season – Callum Sweeney
Coaches' Player Of The Season – Reece O'Brien
Most Improved Player – Lewis Speare
Most Points For The Season – Jared Knowles

Unsung Hero – Morgan Busby

Under 16s
Players' Player Of The Season – Jaxon Kirk - Jones
Coaches' Player Of The Season – Sam Daintith
Most Improved Player– Alfie Gilhooley
Most Points For The Season – Liam Yarwood
Unsung Hero – Sam Hockey

Under 18s
Players' Player Of The Season – Joel Bark
Coaches' Player Of The Season – Jake Meehan
Most Improved Player – Ellis Mahar
Most Points For The Season – Luke Mullarkey
Unsung Hero – Ben McLellan

Mike Gilbert, head coach of the Wild Academy said:

"Special thanks go to the committee, managers and coaches for all their hard work and dedication through the year - Terry Gray, Danny Cliffe, Debbie Alston, Hannah Walker, Sharon Gray, Chantelle Cliffe, Gary Eddleston, Gemma Hockey, Gareth Davies, Tim Campbell, Michael Speare, Vic Bickerton, Shaun Sillery, Jake Meehan, Phil Pearson and Bill Busby – as well as many more for their efforts.

*****

The Widnes Wild Academy Junior Club operates competitive teams at Under 10, 12, 14, 16 and 18 levels and also runs introduction and training sessions for children of all ages and abilities – boys and girls – from beginners to advanced.

For more information, contact Wild Academy Head Coach Mike Gilbert by email at: mike.gilbert@wildacademy.co.uk or telephone the rink on 0151 420 7930.

The Jon Little Recognition Award - awarded to Jake Meehan and presented by Jon's partner Lynda Bird (photo by Hannah Walker)

The Vernon Neil Hardworker Award - awarded to Ben Roberts (photo by Hannah Walker)

Above left: Lucy London in the game officials booth before a Widnes Wild home match during the 2019/20 season. Above right: A cartoon version of Lucy by Manga Mark.

Lucy presenting Howard Hughes with a CD copy of the song that she wrote for the Riverside Raiders team. (Photo by Paul Breeze)

Lucy the poet comparing warm headgear with Andrew Shutt (Photo by Paul Breeze)

Lucy London – Poet In Residence

Lucy London was appointed honorary "Poet In Residence" for the Widnes Wild club in September 2017 and has since made it her mission to immortalise their exploits in verse.

She had previously watched ice hockey for a number of years at Peterborough, Altrincham, Blackburn and Blackpool / Cleveleys and has followed the Wild since moving closer to the area in 2015.

Lucy has been an EIHA off-ice game official at Widnes for several seasons, is the match scorer for Riverside Raiders home games and has been the sponsor of the MVP awards for the Wild women's team for the past three seasons. Unfortunately, she has been laid low by poor health recently and is currently supporting from a distance.

Lucy is an experienced writer and broadcaster and has had two volumes of her own poems published as well as a song book, numerous short stories and various feature articles.

She has also become a bit of an authority on lesser known poetry of the First World War since being asked to put together an exhibition of women poets for the Wilfred Owen Story museum in Birkenhead back in 2012.

She has since edited and published numerous books on the subject of women poets, inspirational women and forgotten male poets of World War One and has staged exhibitions across the UK and in Ireland, France and the USA.

Back in September 2017, it was thought to be the first time that an ice rink had appointed a Poet In Residence and it is just another example that helps reinforce Widnes Wild's commitment to building strong links across the wider community.

Lucy London has a dedicated Facebook page for her poetry residency at Planet Ice Widnes and is keen to encourage other people to explore and develop their own artistic and literary talents.

You can follow her poetic musings on the goings on at Widnes at www.facebook.com/Lucy-Poet-In-Residence

And find information about Lucy's other First World War projects and other publications here: http://femalewarpoets.blogspot.co.uk/

Lucy doing the match scoring at a Riverside Raiders game at Widnes during summer 2018 (Photo by Paul Breeze)

Widnes Wild Poems by Lucy London
Season 2021/22

Ice hockey is coming back!
Widnes Wild on the attack -
Zig zagging round the ice pads -
Widnes Wild the likely lads.

Lucy - Poet in Residence, 2nd July 2021

Hurray Hurray! Here's some Good news today -
Mikey Gilbert, King Ken and Dani Haid
Are all coming back to Widnes Wild to play.
They were part of the team that surely put the Wild
Into Widnes! Let's go Widnes Wild Ice Hockey Team
Your faithful fans are living the dream.

Lucy - Poet in Residence, 26th June 2021

Another piece of Wild good news
Is the return of our Bez Hughes
(With thanks to my ever-patient Muse…)

Lucy - Poet in Residence, 6th July 2021

Widnes Wild are back on ice – for going to games it's been a while
The Wild's new fixture list will make Wild Ones smile
But PLEASE take care and protect those you hold dear
Wild Covid advice you will find here:

Lucy - Poet in Residence, September 2021

Widnes Wild are in action this coming weekend
Widnes Wild have a reputation to defend
For Widnes Wild Ice Hockey Team were the proud winners
Of the prestigious Cups NIHL North and the First Division
On Saturday the Wild face the Blackburn Hawks away
They're at home at Planet Ice to Whitley Warriors on Sunday.

Lucy - Poet in Residence, 9.9.2021

Not just a zip – une fermeture éclaire –
More a way of life in everything we wear.
More than just a zip – you assist Wild's winning ways
Thank you YKK – your sponsorship is ace.

Lucy - Poet in Residence, October 2021

Why not go along and see
Action from the Wild Academy
Entrance to their matches is free.

Lucy - Poet in Residence, 14.11.2021

Alice sends you all loads of love -
She says it's Wild Women she's thinking of
She hopes you all enjoy the match
And wishes she was there to watch.

Lucy - Poet in Residence, 21.11.2021
(Alice is the self-appointed mascot of the Widnes Wild Women's Ice Hockey Team...)

Well done to one of Wild Academy's Ice Hockey Teams
The Widnes Wild Under Fourteens
For scoring the first competitive goal against Leeds
I'm sure this is the first of many such amazing deeds.

Lucy - Poet in Residence, 23.11.2021

Widnes Wild Ice Hockey Team's Teddy Toss for children who are ill
In hospital at Christmas Time – a teddy will sweeten the pill –
At YKK-sponsored Wild home game on 28th November 2021
At Planet Ice in Widnes - you're sure to have lots of fun.

Lucy - Poet in Residence, 23.11.2021

Oh dear me Wild Ones – I've just heard the news -
Covid for Christmas – not something I would choose.
Oh my goodness Wild Ones – what rotten luck -
Covid for Christmas – I'd rather have turkey or duck.
Thinking of you all and sending a healing hug.

Lucy - Poet in Residence, 23rd December 2021

Girls and boys come out to play
Ice hockey – hip hooray!
The Wild Men won away
The Women lost but have upped their game
Win or lose, Wild, we love you just the same.

Lucy - Poet in Residence, 9th February 2022

Shout out to all fans of Widnes Wild:
This is not time to be meek and mild -
It's Time to go Wild! Time to go Wild!
As the Wild are off to the city of Marmalade
Where an important match is to be played.

Lucy - Poet in Residence, 18th February 2022

YKK Widnes Wild face another busy weekend :
On Saturday to Solway Firth their way they wend
On Sunday they play at their home ice rink again
At Planet Ice in Widnes versus Solihull Barons
Play up! Play up! Wonderful Widnes Wild Ones.

Lucy - Poet in Residence, 11 March 2022

On Sunday, 3rd April 2022
Widnes Wild Men are off to face Billingham Stars in the Moralee
Division – that will definitely be an exciting match to see.
Meanwhile, back at the camp, the Wild Women have a match
So if you're at a loose end, why not go along and watch?

Lucy - Poet in Residence, 2.4.2022

Final game of the Moralee Division Season
Sunday 10th April – another good reason
To go and watch Widnes Wild (sponsored by YKK)
As against Sheffield Scimitars they play.

Lucy - Poet in Residence, 8.4.2022

This season's been a roller-coaster ride
For the YKK sponsored Widnes Wild
Today they're away against the Stars of Billingham
(The only rhyme I could find for that is Gillingham...).
On Sunday they host Billingham Stars at Planet Ice
I hope the Wild beat the Stars twice.

Lucy - Poet in Residence, 15.4.2022

Fare you well Rebecca Clayton - known to Wild fans as Bex -
Thank you and good luck for whatever you do next.

Lucy - Poet in Residence, 24th April 2022

Although the season's over there's still lots of Widnes Wild news
So there are still ice hockey challenges for me and my muse.
Matty Barlow and Mikey Gilbert have been called to serve Team
England Under 23 for matches versus Denmark – living the dream.

Lucy - Poet in Residence, 24th April 2022

Well done Wild Academy Under Tens Ice Hockey Team
You have set the bar very high at a really difficult time
Keep up the good work, continue to B Y B
As through the Wild Age Group Teams you climb.

Lucy -Poet in Residence, May 2022

Here we are at the end of another ice hockey season
And to celebrate Widnes Wild have very good reason.
Finishing third in a higher Division
Is not something to treat with derision.
So get your tickets now for a fabulous celebration –
A buffet, then awards and presentations.

Lucy - Poet in Residence, 12.5.2022

*Lucy with Pukka the Penguin
at a Widnes Wild game,
along with some of the toys
that feature in her book "The
Adventures of Bunny, Archie,
Alice & Friends"*

(Photo by Paul Breeze)

Also from Lucy London….

Artists Of The First World War

Guns & Pencils

Purple Patches

The Adventures of Bunny, Archie, Alice & Friends

Female Poets V1

Female Poets V2

No Woman's Land

Aviator Poets & Writers

The Somme 1916

Arras, Messines, Passchendaele

Women Casualties – Belgium & France

Poets' Corners In Foreign Fields

Wilfred Owen: Centenary

Lucy London Songbook

Blackpool to Bond Street

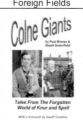

Colne Giants

All available from www.poshupnorth.com, Amazon, Kindle, and all other quality outlets…!

NORTH / SOUTH DIVIDE
WHY NOT COLLECT THE SET?

North / South Divide: The Original

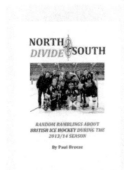

The 2013/14 season was a watershed year for me ice hockey wise. The Fylde Flyers team finished, leaving me with only recreational hockey to write about in Blackpool so I decided to branch out and cover the English National League in a more general manner.

What you will find in this book is a mixture of opinion columns written for Blueliner.com and round-ups and news items that started off on bestkeptsecrets and, after January 2014, ended up on icehockeyreview.co.uk. I hope that makes sense – it shouldn't be boring, anyway…!

ISBN: 9798563183759

Volume 2: Ice Hockey And Me

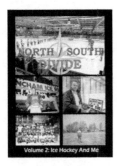

Mainly autobiographical and featuring random and bizarre topics such as:

How I came to be at the World Championships in Luxembourg,
The day I met Stewart Roberts,
Which Sims twin is which and
The story behind Lucy's "French And Ormes" poem...

ISBN: 9781909643451

Volume 3: Cricket & Baseball

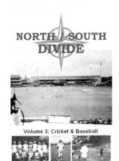

More autobiography - mainly about my involvement in cricket and baseball – plus a few other things as well.

So, just to whet your appetite, in this volume you can read all about:
Why I wasn't any good at cricket at school
The Cricket World Cup in 1999
The Preston Bobcats league baseball team
The Preston University student team of 1996/97
And my experiences of baseball coaching at Summer Camps in the Czech Republic.

ISBN: 9781909643468

COMPANION VOLUME 4
"FRANCE ACTUALLY"
(nothing to do with ice hockey in this one, by the way....)

North / South Divide – Volume 4

ISBN-13: 978-1-909643-47-5

Available now by mail order from Amazon, Posh Up North, Waterstones, Book Depository and all other quality outlets.

COMPANION VOLUME 5
The Bachelor Pad Years

(not much ice hockey in this one either – but still a good read!)

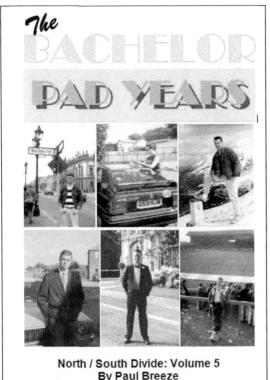

North / South Divide: Volume 5
By Paul Breeze

ISBN-13: 978-1-909643-48-2

Full Contents List:
Preamble: Girls At School, Girl Friends and Girlfriends
1984: Literally!
September 1989: Amsterdam
1990: Welcome To The Bachelor Pad
Spring 1990: Caribbean Interlude
April 1990: Drupa Exhibition
May 1990: Berlin
May 1990: Amsterdam 2
Belinda Carlisle / Erasure/ The Stranglers & Other Musical Memories
August 1990: Paul Gets A Car
September 1990: Polish Pursuits 1 – Trip To Zakopane
Autumn 1990: Nordic No Go
April / May 1991: Polish Pursuits 2 - Visit To Warsaw
1991: A Little Bit Of Lynda
Autumn 1991: Whitney Houston & Roxette
September 1991: Inter Rail
December 1991: Chris Rea / Spain
Squash 1985-1995
Football In The Bachelor Pad Years
Ice Hockey In The Bachelor Pad Years
1992-93: The Bachelor Pad Mk2, Preston
1992 & 93: Jola In England

Available by Mail Order from Amazon, Posh Up North, Waterstones, Book Depository and all other quality outlets.

Schooldays

A Stanground Upbringing

VOLUME 6

Schooldays

A Stanground Upbringing

ISBN: 978-1-909643-49-9

North / South Divide - Volume 6

Above: PB standing around looking "expectant" at the Laidler Play Off weekend in Widnes in April 2019 (Photo by Fiona Haggar)

ABOUT THE AUTHOR: Paul Breeze

Registered EIHA Off Ice Game Official

Official match announcer for Widnes Wild NIHL matches (2017-2020) and Wild women's team matches (2017-date)

Available for games at Deeside and Widnes ice rinks.

7 days' notice appreciated

Recreational matches & charity games a speciality.

EIHA Involvement

UK Anti Doping 2021 Code Module (01/21)

EIHA Manager's Course (08/20)

EIHA Re-Activate Covid-19 Awareness Course (08/20)

EIHA GDPR Course (08/20)

UK Anti Doping Clean Sport Advisor Course (09/20)

UK Anti Doping Coach Clean Course (09/20)

Media Panel Member for NIHL North Player of the Month Award - seasons 2017/8 and 2019/20

Former member of British Ice Hockey Writers Association (BIHWA) and Ice Hockey Journalists UK (IHJUK)

International

November 1999: Media facilities adviser to tournament director Frank Dempster for the Team GB Pool A IIHF Qualifying tournament at Sheffield Arena.

April 1998: Covered IIHF European Junior Championships Pool D, Luxembourg, for local radio and written press.

NIHL Play Offs

2019: Match announcer for NIHL Laidler Division Play Off Weekend

2019: Presentations photographer for Play Off weekend

2018: Match announcer for NIHL Laidler Division Play Off Weekend

Widnes Wild NIHL Team

2016 – date: Match reports and news items for Widnes Wild NIHL team for website and local press.

2017-2020: Match announcer for Wild NIHL games at Widnes

Occasional music and photos to cover as required

October 2017: Post - match interviews for BASN's "Drop The Puck" TV programme, broadcast on "Made In Liverpool" TV channel and elsewhere

Widnes Wild Ladies Team

2021/22: Official EGS scorer for Wild Ladies team home games

2017-date: match announcer

2018-date: official MVP trophy sponsor

2017-date: post match presentation photos (as required)

2015-date: Match reports and news items for Widnes Wild women's team for websites and local press.

Widnes Wild Junior Academy

2018-date: Match reports and news items for U10, U12, U14, U16 and U18 teams for website and local press.

British Para Ice Hockey League

2017-date: Match announcer for Mayhem sledge hockey games at Widnes

2017-date: match and league reports for press and websites

September 2018: Match announcer and statistician for British Para Ice Hockey League play off weekend at Widnes

Recreational Ice Hockey

Since 2021: Admin Manager for North West Lions tournament team

2017-19 Match announcer & music for Riverside Raiders rec games

2017-2019: Website and press reports for Riverside Raiders, Widnes Wildcats and Halton Huskies rec matches

2017/18: Match announcer & music for Halton Huskies rec games

July 2019: Match announcer for Wyre Seagulls v Flintshire Phantoms Summer Classic match at Widnes

June 2019: Scorer for Blackburn Buccaneers v Riverside Raiders Summer Classic match at Deeside

July 2018: Match Announcer & music, timekeeper and scorer for Planet Ice Rec Tournament weekend

January (8th) 2017: Announcer for Antony Morris Memorial Cup charity game at Widnes

June (26th) 2016: Announcer for Bob Kenyon Memorial Shield charity game at Deeside. Also produced souvenir match programme.

Summer 2013: Produced souvenir match programme for the Deeside Dragons v Liverpool Leopards Legends game at Deeside.

Cleveleys / Blackpool

2014/15: Match announcer for Blackpool Seagulls EIHA 16 North 2 matches at Fylde Coast Ice Arena in Blackpool

2012/13: Match announcer and MC for Blackpool Seagulls home games at SubZero ice arena in Cleveleys during 2012/13 - also produced match programmes and musical accompaniment.

2011-13: Match reports and news items for Fylde Flyers ENL team

Early Days

1998/99: Stand in goal judge and occasional timekeeper at Altrincham Aces ENL matches

August 1998: Volunteer at Trafford Tournament, Altrincham

Summer 1992: A few training sessions with Eric Cregan and the Blackpool junior team at Blackpool Ice Drome

1988 - 1990: Rather unnoticeable 3rd line stint as a rec player at Peterborough - (Total career stat: 1 assist...).

January 1983: Saw first ice hockey match in Peterborough - became hooked!

Radio CV

Radio presenter on 103.2 Preston FM from April 2009 to November 2014

also appeared on – or produced content for - Wireless Radio.biz, Fylde FM, East Lancs Radio and NIHL Radio internet broadcasting stations.

Radio presenter on 106FM Resort Radio, Blackpool, during October 1998

Radio presenter on 107FM Radio Waky/ Programme Europe 2, Luxembourg, 1997 to 1998

Radio presenter on Blackpool's Kit Kat Radio 1996-1999

A typical view of PB at a game at Widnes in 2018. Everybody else is watching the action while I am concentrating on what the clock is doing... In this photo left to right: Lucy, PB, Gill Gillingham (Scorer), Andrew Shutt (timekeeper) and Matt Lloyd (Penalty Box Judge) (Photo by David Tattum)

Above left: presenting a highly contentious box of chocolates as an MVP award to Wild women's Sav Sumner (Photo by Geoff White) Above right: PB in typical multi-tasking mode at a women's game – announcing the MVPs from the middle of the ice so as to be able to take the photos as well. (Photo by Andrew Shutt)

Match announcer for a Blackpool Seagulls game at SubZero in Cleveleys in 2012

Paul and Lucy presenting the match puck to captain Wayne Whitby for a Fylde Flyers home game at the Subzero rink in Cleveleys, 2012. (Photo by Mick Caunce)

Above left: Scorer's bench at Altrincham Aces, 1998/99

Above right: lake ice hockey in Germany, January 1997

Left: Kit Kat Radio in Blackpool, Summer 1997

Above left: Presenting the match puck at John Lawless's testimonial match Peterborough Pirates v Fife Flyers, December 1986. Above right: Playing in a rec charity game at Peterborough, March 1990 (Photos by Francis Page).

ICE HOCKEY BOOKS BY STUART LATHAM

ISBN	Title	RRP £
9781838116507	60 Years Of The Altrincham Aces	£15.99
9781838116521	Ice Hockey in Bristol	£15.99
9781838116538	The Deeside Dragons	£15.99
9781838116545	The Manchester Storm	£15.99
9781838116569	The Rise and Fall of the Manchester Phoenix	£15.99
9781838116590	The Cardiff Devils	£16.99
9781838332808	Ice Hockey Memories	£18.99
9781838332822	The History of the Slough Jets	£17.99
9781838332846	More Ice Hockey Memories	£17.99
9780953060863	Blood Sweat and Tears Ice Hockey in Peterborough	£24.99
9780953060870	Swindon Wildcats 1986-2016	£22.99
9780953060887	The History of the Bracknell Bees	£24.99
9781838332853	Ice Hockey in Edinburgh	£18.99
9781838332891	Stars Wars- The Oxford City Stars	£16.99
9781838460907	Swindon Ice Hockey Statistically Speaking 1986-2021	£17.99
9781838460914	In Their Own Words - Swindon Ice Hockey Memories	£16.99
9781838460938	Hockey in Haringey	£17.99
9781838460952	Ice Hockey In Solihull	£18.99

Available by mail order from Waterstones.com, brownbfs.co.uk, foyles.co.uk and other major outlets.

For more details, contact
stuartlatham65@sky.com or tel: +44 7702035951

231

INTERESTING WEBSITES

If you have found any of this in the least bit interesting, you might like to have the occasional look at some of these various websites which, as of Summer 2022, I am currently involved with:

Check out our audio and video archive in our dedicated "Paul & Lucy's Best Kept Secrets" YouTube channel at www.youtube.com.

www.icehockeyreview.co.uk

NIHL Yearbook Back Issues Available

*Available by mail order from www.poshupnorth.com,
Amazon, icehockeyreview.co.uk and other quality outlets*

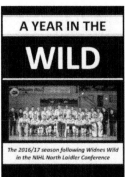
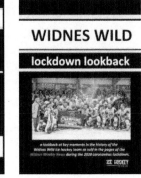

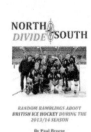
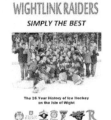
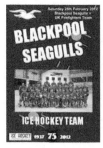

WIDNES WILD
LOCKDOWN LOOKBACK

WIDNES WILD

lockdown lookback

a lookback at key moments in the history of the Widnes Wild ice hockey team as told in the pages of the Widnes Weekly News during the 2020 coronavirus lockdown.

ICE HOCKEY

A lookback at key moments in the history of the Widnes Wild ice hockey team as told in the pages of the Widnes Weekly News during the 2020 coronavirus lockdown.

Packed with photos, interviews and fascinating stories.

ISBN: 9781909643406

Full Contents List:

Questions for the Chairman

Widnes Wild's First Ever Game

Richard Charles Looks Back At The First Widnes Game

Where Are They Now?

Craig Williams And The First Ever Widnes Wild Goal

Widnes Wild In The End Of Season Play Offs

Widnes Wild In the End of Season Play Offs – Part Two

Widnes Wild In The Promotion Game

Wild Imports – Then & Now

Widnes Wild In The NIHL Cup

Widnes Wild's Title Winning Season

Widnes Wild At The National Championship Game

Ken Armstrong – 200 Games And Counting

Tom Jackson's Widnes Wild Appearance Record

Mike Mawer Reaches 100 Game Milestone

Dan Bracegirdle Looks Back Over 100 Games

Widnes / Deeside Rivalry – Part 1

Widnes / Deeside Rivalry – Part 2

Widnes / Altrincham Rivalry

Widnes & Blackburn – Head To Head

Wild Break Records In Blackburn

Wild Go To Hull And Back

NIHL Player Award Winners

Available by mail order from www.poshupnorth.com, Amazon, icehockeyreview.co.uk and other quality outlets